Taking the
TIME
to
LOVE

Taking the
TIME
to
LOVE

Joseph McCarthy

ThomasMore®
– An RCL Company –
Allen, Texas

Send all inquiries to:

THOMAS MORE PUBLISHING
200 East Bethany Drive
Allen, Texas 75002-3804

Telephone: 800-264-0368 / 972-390-6300

Fax: 800-688-8356 / 972-390-6560

E-mail: **cservice@rcl-enterprises.com**

Website: **www.ThomasMore.com**

Printed in the United States of America

Library of Congress Catalog Number: 2002109867

7496   ISBN 0-88347-496-4

1 2 3 4 5   06 05 04 03 02

Contents

Foreword

May You Be So Blessed!

DEAR READER,

It is truly a privilege for us to introduce you to Joe McCarthy's book, *Taking the Time to Love*. We feel like hosts at a good party helping to bring new friends together. But we should also give you an alert: *Beware!* You are about to encounter some profound meditations that will engage you to the marrow bone and challenge you to change your life. Joe will call attention to your patterns of life and relationship with riveting reflections of critique and hope. At least, this is what Joe does for us, every time we meet.

Not that we meet that often or for that long—being too caught up in the busyness that Joe names so well. Yet, we always come away changed. We know of no one who has a keener sense of the dire straits that face Americans as a people and our desperate need for a radical reordering of priorities—for our own sakes and for the life of the world. Joe sounds a clarion call that lest we destroy it all—God's great human experiment—we must change our ways across the board, on the personal, inter-personal, and political levels, in every nook and cranny of our lives.

We also come away from Joe feeling bamboozled and amused, confronted and befuddled, engaged and entertained. You will, too. We suspect that it's his powerful combination of the prophetic and poetic. Joe is a radical prophet and a raw poet, much in the tradition of an Isaiah or Jeremiah, aye, with deep echoes of the Carpenter of Nazareth. And like the great prophets of old, he offers both criticism and hope. Though the doomsday clock is ticking—even running fast—we need not settle for our "toys are us"—we can let go of our idols and let God's law of love rule our lives.

To be with Joe is an experience of "real presence." He helps us to remember that God is ever with us and that we should live accordingly, doing God's will for fullness of life "on earth as it is in heaven." And for years we've urged, "Joe, you must publish for a wider audience." His room is literally littered with scraps of paper, all with jottings of gems that deserve to be recorded and widely read. And we've invariably said coming home in the car, "What a loss that Joe doesn't put that stuff out as a book."

At last, here it is!

Like Joe's conversations, there is no obvious beginning, middle, or end. You can jump in just about anywhere, move forward or circle back around, reread or push on. But take your time; savor Joe's meditations; let them worm their way into your heart. This is how *Taking the Time to Love* will change your consciousness and then your commitments—for life for all. At least, this is how we invariably experience our friend Joe.

May you be so blessed!

Professors Thomas Groome and Colleen Griffith
Boston College

What's It All About?

*Surely, this commandment that I am commanding you
today is not too hard for you, nor is it too far away. . . .
No, the word is very near to you; it is in your mouth and in
your heart for you to observe* (Deuteronomy 30:11, 14).

A YOUNG FATHER SAYS: "I am out to work in the morning
before the kids get up and when I get home at night the kids are
in bed. My wife works too. I am so afraid my children will grow
up not knowing their parents."

The *Time of no time all the time* for the people we love is our
most agonizing problem. Our normal day is packed with action.

We do for each other.
We give to each other.
We pick each other up.
We drop each other off.

But we're always in such a hurry in our heads that we see
each other only sideways. We don't have time to enter deeply
into each other's inner happenings.

Our American way of life, the way we love to live, is a way of
thinking, feeling, and acting.

It's a pace!
It's a style!
It's a way of doing things!
It's a way of getting things done.

Our highways are our homes. Our wheels are our shoes. We are always on the road; we are always on the go. What makes us American is the pace at which we travel—the pressures that pressure us, the stresses that stress us all penciled into our schedules:

Numberless projects,
Endless irons in the fire,
Many hats on one head,
Pulled at once in many directions,
Driven in so many ways.

We find ourselves beginning to resent having to put out more energy than our bodies have to give. Dancing as fast as we can, we are dancing too fast; we are no longer keeping up the pace.

Fax machines, cellular phones, laptop computers, pagers, beepers—all our time-saving devices have outstripped our human ability to stay on top of things. We limited human beings are no longer a match for our high-tech age. Our mechanical creations are now in charge of us. They own us. They run our lives. The net result: we have lost control.

Frustrated, defeated, depleted, exhausted—anger is leaking out everywhere, from all of us. We have gone from *God Bless America* to become God's very angry people.

We're all in a rage—Air Rage, Road Rage, Work Rage, Desk Rage, Home Rage—our way of life has followed us home and we find ourselves taking out our frustrations on the ones we love most.

In our living rooms, in our bedrooms, in our children's rooms—this is where the hurting is happening. We are paying an awful price in our relationships for the awful clip at which we live. Our families are our hurting place.

The missing piece in all our hurry is that we no longer have time for ourselves. We no longer take time for one another. We no longer find time for love.

The upside of our way of life is the abundant harvest of commercial goods we all enjoy. Whatever our hearts desire, our wallets can buy. The downside of our way of life, however, is that making enough money to buy everything we want is eating up all of our time.

Faced with the ever-rising cost of everything, just functioning takes all the energy we have to give. We have reached a state of immobility. We are in over our heads. We will never catch up. We are stuck in the revolving doors of a self-defeating system called credits and debts.

And to blame others for what's going on, to expect others to right what's wrong, is a childlike response to what's happening. No president, no government, no political party, no budget, can do for us now what each one of us must do for ourselves— namely, change our lifestyle totally, give top priority to our relationships by factoring into our schedules plenty of time for love.

The time for change has come, not gone. Whatever has gone wrong, it is something we are doing to ourselves. The source of most of our problems lies in the exchange we have made by trading off people for gadgets and goods.

- We are the ones who buy up all the timesaving devices and then spend all our time paying for them.

- We are the ones who move away from the company of others to play alone with our videocassettes, our compact disc players, our personal computers.

- We are the ones responsible for shifting the focus of our lives away from human beings to luxuries, amenities, and comforts.

- We are the ones who have made far too much of our drapes matching our rugs, and the towels in our bathrooms matching the colors of our bathroom walls.

- We are the ones who have allowed our simple down-to-earth needs for food and water, clothes and shelter, to become blown out of proportion into a mountain of products so that the merchandise now becomes a wedge between ourselves and ourselves, and ourselves and one another.

What is radically wrong with the way we live, simply put, is this: All the things we buy and give to one another can never ever make up to them for not being there with them ourselves.

What's lost and left out of our lives in the fast lane is time for listening, time for talking, time to be with the people we love. Something is horribly wrong with the way we have organized our lives if to maintain our standard of living we have to put our loved ones on hold. What's left of our lives?

We must never forget that the primary commodity we humans seek, need, or long for is the close connection and intimate contact with those we love the most.

Products, profits, merchandise—these are not what life is all about.

It is love that makes life.
It is love that makes love.

Taking the Time to Love

It is love that makes us whole,
Love given out totally,
Love taken in totally,
Love given back totally.

Life's longed-for dream has always been giving ourselves away to others and having ourselves returned. The gift of self to others is the gift that God intends. Self-esteem, self-worth, is something none of us can ever give ourselves. Our sense of self comes to us as a gift from those who give us love. Love is told to us no other way except by those who *take the time to hang in there with us day by day by day.*

The most exciting moments in our otherwise dull existence is this give and take of love that reciprocates back and forth between us human beings.

The nature of our human nature is that this love is essential to us. We may be able to hurry everything else, but we cannot hurry love. We must take time to find each other. We humans take time to be found. It takes a lifetime to say we know each other well.

Making the time,
Taking the time,
To tell our loved one,
They are worth our time—
This is what life is all about.
This is what's real.
This is all that's real.
This is what God sends us here to do.

Life is love.
Love takes time.
And this is what time is for.

And yet time for love
Is what we have
Such a great big lack of.
Life was never meant to be this way!

So we journey back into the story of our American story to better understand how we became the way we have become, buried alive as we are under an avalanche of commercial goods.

" *'You shall love the Lord your God with all your heart, and with all your soul, and with all your mind.' This is the greatest and first commandment. And a second is like it: 'You shall love your neighbor as yourself.' On these two commandments hang all the law and the prophets"* (Matthew 22:37–38).

We Are Made for Family

For my thoughts are not your thoughts,
nor are your ways my ways, says the LORD.
For as the heavens are higher than the earth,
so are my ways higher than your ways
and my thoughts than your thoughts (Isaiah 55:8–9).

AMERICA IS A STORY told ever so briefly of how everyday men and everyday women, with nothing at all but a passionate faith in the works of their hands and a God-given trust in their own human worth, built a new world out of this land. The story of our American story is the story of answered prayers. It is the story of dreams come true.

America began from humble beginnings. Starting out with nothing at all America wound up having it all. Efforts met with success; progress progressed; expressways connected to expressways and became interstate highways. The fast lane became the image of who we are.

As the pace picked up, love thinned out. In the movement of progress over the years, America concentrated more and more away from people and more and more on money and things.

Shopping malls rose as big as small towns—rows and rows of stores, ceiling to floor, wall to wall, filled with things our money could buy. As our needs increased, as our wants multiplied, before we knew it, with the passage of time, we had all become slaves to our economics, nonstop shoppers. Now taking a living from our world is taking up all of our time.

Abundance is a blessing, but abundance has brought upon us many problems of its own. We live in a blitz of merchandise and goods, in a world where people no longer have time for people.

Home alone, our latchkey kids, like ourselves, have a house full of toys and no one to play with. Our gain in consumer goods has become our loss in human connection. This is the dark side of where we find ourselves.

We Americans have not always been so buried alive in material goods. Back in the 1920s, 1930s, and early 1940s, we were a nation of neighborhoods, a people centered on people. Our homes were full of families; our streets were full of friends. We knew everyone; everyone knew us. Way back then, without knowing it, we were what we took for granted; we were a community.

Since the end of World War II all that has changed. After the war there was affluence for everyone who worked, and everyone began to work. The late 1940s into the 1950s and early 1960s brought prosperity, opportunities, and upward mobility in our society. As the paychecks got bigger, buying power increased, luxuries became necessities for everyone.

From house to house, from town to town, all across America, televisions blared away, painting pictures for us of a new reality. Advertising was in its heyday making "have-to-haves" out of non-necessities.

We never asked how much stuff we needed; we never looked at what junk we got. In the pursuit of happiness we felt it was within our bill of rights to have it all. What was bigger was better; what was new was great; the latest was always the best. We grew tired of old things fast. We always needed new things to make life hum.

Life became more manufactured and more artificial as we became more compulsive in our galloping needs to have it all. But the addictive nature of our acquisitive behavior remained invisible to us. Our fascination with cash and pricey things became habit-forming, setting up inside us a hidden force that put a wedge between ourselves and ourselves, and a wall between ourselves and others.

As the things we bought and sold became more refined and better finished, we ourselves became more surly and cold-blooded with one another. Life inside us and life between us got crossed out of our busy schedules.

As Americans we were always good workers, and so we worked our fingers to the bone to bring the money home. But the price of keeping up kept going up. The more we worked the more we fell behind, always just one paycheck away from loss of credit.

Making money in our sleep, the menacing shadows of our bills kept appearing on our bedroom walls. Overwrought by overwhelming debts, the strain on everyone overworked showed up in frayed nerves and short fuses. With everyone stretched beyond their strength, marriages broke from overload. Love in America was stamped "out of order" because life in America was out of focus.

And here we are today, some of us working two jobs, both parents working in most households, life reduced to working and being tired. Caregivers and providers at once, we wind up in a *terrible* bind. Inside we are caught in a tug of war—pulled between people and things, the things we want to buy and own and the people we would like to love.

The *Time of no time all the time* for the ones we love, is our most basic problem. And unless we grabble with this issue we are faced with the disintegration of our families and the gradual but inevitable breakdown of America.

> *"No one can serve two masters; for a slave will either hate the one and love the other, or be devoted to the one and despise the other. You cannot serve God and wealth"* (Matthew 6:24).

Off to Work I Go!

The heart is devious above all else;
it is perverse—
who can understand it?
I the LORD test the mind
and search the heart,
To give to all according to their ways,
according to the fruit of their doings
(Jeremiah 17:9–10).

THE BAD NEWS is that something is horribly wrong with our way of life.

The good news is that we ourselves can fix it. The solution to all our hurting dilemmas is so simple: *Stop Shopping!*

In the enormous economic complexity of the international marketplace, it sounds mad and terribly naïve to suggest that what's basically wrong with America would turn out right if we all boycotted our shopping malls.

Again and again it is our manic, willful overspending in relentless, madcap screw-loose shopping that locks us into a prison of our own making, always squeezed for money and always pressed for time. Shopping is its own punishment.

It is shopping that keeps us working forever.
It is shopping that keeps us forever at school.
It is shopping that keeps us forever in debt.

Life in the shopping lane makes for life in the traffic lane. Our lifestyle demands our work style. Our work style supports our lifestyle.

Once we diagnose shopping as the illness we suffer, then all the dominoes fall. Money, school, work—those aspects of our life that consume so much of our time are all held hostage to our unstoppable shopping habits.

Enough is never enough; enough will never do in our fast, efficient, commercial world. Life in the shopping lane wants and wants and wants for more and more and more.

The steps of the dance we all move through in our shopping sprees are these.

Step 1: We see something we like and we say to ourselves "I want to own that."

Step 2: We go ahead and buy it, but we buy it on credit, and then we are owned by what we own.

Step 3: When we want to own too many things, we wind up owing too much.

Step 4: The price tag for owning so much is that we wind up owned body and soul by the company we work for to pay off what we owe on what we own.

A bumper sticker says it well:

I owe, I owe, I owe
So off to work I go,
Two jobs now have I,

I pay, I pay, I pay,
The Bank reclaimed my house today
Homeless now am I.
I cry, I cry, I cry.
No one came to say goodbye.

Living the American way, shopping the American style, we don't always wind up enjoying the American dream. Freedom no longer feels like freedom when we are straddled with bills and mortgaged for life.

"Do not seek your own advantage, but that of
the other. . . . whatever you do, do everything for
the glory of God" (1 Corinthians 10:24, 31).

Life Is for Living

But this is the covenant that I will make with the house of Israel after those days, says the LORD: I will put my law within them, and I will write it on their hearts; I will be their God, and they shall be my people (Jeremiah 31:33).

IN OUR HURRY to nowhere we are squandering ourselves on the wrong priorities. Shopping is hijacking everything else in our lives.

The long hours we work are never enough!
The wages we earn are never enough!
The education we get is never enough
to keep up with the high cost
of the high standard of living.

Our high standard of living is too damn high when it comes between ourselves and ourselves and ourselves and the ones we love.

There is a great "not at home-ness" in the way we now live. Our households become motels of overnight stays. We leave the light on for one another. Cars come, cars go, people shower and change their clothes. They leave fast. We don't hang out together very long.

After a while, when we make no time for talking and lack the time for listening, we go into hiding. We wind up living together with the closest of strangers.

The space between us may be small but the distance is very great when everyone around us is always in a hurry. We meet but miss each other. We make contact but do not connect. We come together but do not relate. We deal with each other from the outside. We leave each other out. It is hard to find love in a world where no one has time.

What compounds our problems and increases the distance that has grown between us are gadgets of entertainment we bring home with us when we go out shopping.

Behind the closed doors of our own rooms in solitary confinement we are headlocked into the Internet. We are head-setted into our stereo systems. We watch our own videos, with our own video players. We talk to our own friends on our own cellular phones.

The sorry thing we are doing to our loved ones is that we are hanging up on one another to hang out by ourselves in our own cyber space playground.

Life as we now live it has radically shifted from human relationships to electronic gadgets. We have more information, less conversation; more communication, less companionship. We are more electronically connected, and more emotionally alone.

Technology has done wonders for humankind. It makes everything possible except closeness to others. Individuals in families now live in seclusion.

Comparing our human past with our human present, we must acknowledge that a new human world has come into existence. As our relationships to gadgets has grown stronger, our ties with each other has diminished. We have swapped human company for the pleasure we get out of things.

Fish don't see the sea; ants never see an anthill; bees never see a beehive—neither can we see through this all-encompassing commercial world we have come to live. Massive as the sun, everywhere like the sky, we live under an all-persistent, pervasive climate of hustlers, hawkers, and hookers, seducing us into being shoppers, buyers, and customers.

Shopping 'til we drop has us working 'til we're dead, in hock over our heads, and handcuffed to the hands of the clock. Shopping is the central force shaping, determining, dictating, controlling everything else in our lives, informing us constantly that the point of our existence is found no longer in persons but in our personal possessions.

What does it profit them if they gain the whole world, but lose or forfeit themselves? (Luke 9:25)

Growing Up in America

". . . you saw how the LORD your God carried you, just as one carries a child, all the way that you traveled until you reached this place" (Deuteronomy 1:31).

OUR INFANTILE ENTRANCE into the commercial world happened crawling on all fours up to the television. From early childhood television was our babysitter.

Its images danced in our eyes; its sounds popped in our ears. It was our closest friend; it told us stories and made us laugh. From day one as a child, it was our constant companion, staying with us all day long, telling us how the world works. We saw the world around us as it was shown to us through our audio/video window.

While we were still very young, life was sold to us as buying, getting, and having things. Things to buy, to own, to have, spilled out of the television every day into our living rooms. Psyched by what we saw, we were made fidgety by our wants for what was out there.

Though still barely able to walk, the hype was seeded in us to look to things for life. Wanting everything became an all-consuming appetite.

An alternate world formed inside us as the place of things in our lives took the place of relationships. Slowly but surely, through media influence, the source of our energy shifted away from the importance of our friends to the importance of things.

Our heart, naturally sensitive to persons, became dulled by the spectacular magnificence of all sorts of things out there that we could own and have for ourselves. Very early and very young, we developed an appetite for things that only things can satisfy. It can happen to anyone because it happens to us all.

Growing up in America, we grow up like the world we grew up in—the only world we've ever known. The world where everyone around us talks of little else except *owning, having, getting, buying,* and *selling things.* Commercialism is everywhere all around us; it passes straight into our blood stream and becomes second nature to who we are.

Given the way we are raised, drifting into compulsive shopping seems inevitable. Things are our stimulants and our sedatives, our uppers and our downers, so much so that some of us become so strung out on things to keep us happy that we are addicts before we know it. We use all kinds of commodities as experiences to alter our emotions and play around with our moods.

So here we are today. Our closets are full of clothes; our yards are full of cars; our rooms are full of cutting-edge technologies. Everyone has everything. No one has time for anyone. As Mother Teresa said of us "The poverty of America is the scarcity of time you have for one another."

The stupidest thing we Americans are doing is the premium we place on material goods. The allure of commodity chic has us all in its thrall.

Our whole identity is so intertwined with our lifestyle, our way of life has us by the soul. Slowly but surely we are fast becoming a one-sided, lopsided culture. Shopping is our way of being in the world. Shopping is our national pastime and it's not a harmless hobby. Shopping, the sin we love to commit, is tying us up into conflicted knots.

Things take the place of people.
Money takes the place of love.
Work takes the place of family.
Career takes the place of kids.

Relationships get shoved aside; they get in the way of our doing and having it all. Our habits of shopping and buying make us blind to what's real. In the mad frenetic traffic of it all we are deprived of the precious time we need for a deeply connected, loving relationship.

To make a living, no matter how good a living we make, we abandon one another to maintain our way of life. There is no way we can ever justify the way we have organized our world.

For you did not receive a spirit of slavery to fall back into fear, but you have received a spirit of adoption. When we cry, "Abba! Father!" it is that very Spirit bearing witness with our spirit that we are children of God (Romans 8:15–16).

Our Children
Need Parents

Is not this the fast that I choose:
. . . to share your bread with the hungry
and bring the homeless poor into your house;
when you see the naked, to cover them,
and not to hide yourself from your own kin?
(Isaiah 58:6, 7)

FOR MORE AND MORE children left home alone, life is no
longer life with other children, or other human beings for that
matter. Life is a videotape—life is prerecorded.

This is where we are coming apart. This is where we are
losing it. When those who love us are not there for us, because
they don't have that kind of time to give us, the injuries we
sustain are the wounding of our sense of self.

This is especially so of little children deprived of the caring,
soothing, consistent, reliable, stabilizing, loving presence of a
parent; they are never drawn out of themselves into the wonder-
fully satisfying world of closeness to others.

Deprived of the experience of the good-enough presence
of others, America is spawning a new generation of humans, a

generation whose sense of self is a lot less sure, easily frightened, and very fragmented. Torn asunder by the breaking and brokenness all around them, our children grow up worrying their way through fragile, dangling, unstable relationships.

America's issues are not superficial. Our distress is emotional. Our problems are psychological. Our interior life and life among ourselves gets sidelined because of the way we live.

Our American way of life creates the very opposite environment that we humans need to grow, to flower, to bloom as human beings.

Our American way of life is devastating to our sense of self because it is destroying us all at the most intimate level possible. However glitzy and glossy we appear on the outside [on a multi-media level], on the inside our feelings are scrambled.

Real closeness to others and deep bonding with one another is a time-consuming endeavor that entails an awful lot of talking, an awful lot of listening, an awful lot of being together. This is exactly the kind of time-consuming activity we don't have much time for any more. We need no extra brain cells to tell ourselves our way of life is nonsustainable.

In the next five to ten years, two things are certain, besides death and taxes. With our technological advances in communication gadgets, the pace of life will become even faster. And the amount of products manufactured and marketed will grow even more abundant, feeding the present frenzy and increasing the present momentum. We will then have to work more, to buy more, to have more.

Is this the "more" that we need and want? If it means even less time than we have now for the ones we love, how can we halt the madness except by looking critically at ourselves and what up to now has been going on behind our backs?

The four corner stones of our American living arrangement are money, school, work, and shopping. These four systems feed off each another and feed into each other. Remove shopping from this quadrant and the other three lose their desperate urgency and frenetic intensity.

Cutting down on shopping cuts down on spending, cuts down on needing so much money, cuts down on working overtime all the time, cuts down on our life-long need for further education for further job qualification. Once we question our commercial way of life and say no to shopping as our national pastime, then we open ourselves to an entirely different lifestyle.

"Come to me, all you that are weary and are carrying heavy burdens, and I will give you rest. Take my yoke upon you, and learn from me; for I am gentle and humble in heart, and you will find rest for your souls. For my yoke is easy, and my burden is light" (Matthew 11:28–30).

We Love the Way We Live

By your great wisdom in trade
you have increased your wealth,
and your heart has become proud in your wealth.
Therefore thus says the Lord GOD:
Because you compare your mind
with the mind of a god,
I will bring strangers against you (Ezekiel 28:5–7).

UP UNTIL NOW, we Americans have stumbled along, in a
trance, going along with whatever was going on in our nation.
Believing so much in our American system we never examined
our lives. But now, the slow dawning of a sinking feeling has
come upon us all. Our innocence is gone. Good intentions are
not enough. There is a hex on the way we live. *America does not
feel like family any more!*

Any American thirty years old or older has but to consult his
or her own experience to verify for themselves that a terrible
change is taking place in our land. It is a change that looks an
awful lot more like brokenness, hurting, and disintegration than
wholeness, wellness, or health.

Once we see through our own situation, we are no longer beaten down by the system. The dice are no longer loaded against us; we are free if we choose to create for ourselves a more friendly environment, an environment more conducive to richer and deeper relationships.

There is an alternative. And the alternative is a lifestyle of voluntary simplicity where we make do with an awful lot less, so we can be with one another an awful lot more.

No easy task lies ahead in sorting out and separating necessities from luxuries, eliminating junk and cutting back in spending, to settle into a meaningful, frugal existence.

In the land of the free and the home of the brave it will take an awful lot more religious guts to downsize our standard of living than it took our forbears to upscale their lifestyle into our deluxe way of life.

Our best endeavors are sure to come up against the ironclad fact that our whole identity is tightly padlocked into our way of existing.

We love the way we live, so it is very difficult admitting that our way of life has become unmanageable. It is humbling to acknowledge that we ourselves are hooked for good into our lifestyle. Not until we try to modify our behavior and change the pace at which we travel through life do we realize the chokehold grip it has upon us.

It is only when we try to slow down and give ourselves more time to be with one another that we are faced with the demons inside us that drive us on automatic overdrive, impulses that we

must know
   must do
      must have
         must buy

> *must get*
> > *can't wait*
> > > *got to get there*

These are the fevers and frenzies inside us that power us. These are the traits and the habits of compulsion that drive us. These compulsions are not about to leave us overnight. They are who we are. How frightening it is to realize how close in behavior to addicts is our attraction to commercial products. To keep ourselves happy we need all kinds of commodities to alter our moods. We depend on shopping for our fixes.

All addicts whether they be gamblers, alcoholics, drug addicts, sexaholics, or workaholics have two characteristics in common:

1. *They always hurt themselves.*

2. *They always hurt the ones they love.*

Whether we name our lifestyle an addiction or not does not really matter anymore because the way we now live life is distressfully hurting to ourselves and terribly hurting to the ones we love.

"Blessed are the poor in spirit,
for theirs is the kingdom of heaven" (Matthew 5:3).

Question Time in America

Then the LORD said, "I have observed the misery of my people who are in Egypt; I have heard their cry on account of their taskmasters. Indeed I know their sufferings, and I have come down to deliver them from the Egyptians, and to bring them up out of that land to a good and broad land, a land flowing with milk and honey" (Exodus 3:7–8).

IN THE JACKHAMMER pressure of our everyday frenzy there is no present in our schedule. All of our time is so full of demands, where is there space for the present moment? In our fast-forward, efficient, commercial world, do we even count as persons?

The mistake we have made in our retail-focused extravaganzas is that we have hitched our very families to product-mongering enterprises. We are all being fed as hamburger meat into the global blender of multinational, economic, vending machines. Consolidations, conglomerations, and takeovers have taken us all under one big roof.

We now live in a new empire, faceless and nameless, remote and terrible—up there, out there, somewhere, nowhere, is head-quarters, where no one knows any one. There is no one there. Everything is run by computers. No one is accountable to anyone for what all this is doing to us.

Transnational, international outfits, anonymous marketers above, on top, and outside of us have life-and-death control over our existence, and they do not give a damn for human beings.

Everything is about anything that makes money. We human beings, we persons are of little worth. We are used up and then thrown away like used paper cups.

Living off this set up is everyone's nightmare.

Hard are the laws that bind us, and cruel this system on those who cannot pay their dues. To survive each one of us must keep up the momentum. To lose our edge is to fall behind. To fall behind is a door next door, to the nearest homeless shelter. This is the prospect of terror that hangs like a sword over everyone's head.

We human beings are more vulnerable now than in the days of evil kings and feudal lords. At least back then people had each other. Now we are all alone in a world of no one, run by computers. Life is arranged for us; it is not about us. It owns us; it controls us; it pressures us; it chains us all to the hands of the clock.

Hurry, Hurry, Hurry goes our world. *Zoom, Zoom, Zoom* goes everyone all around us. The pace of life has crossed the line; keeping up to speed is no longer possible. Staying on top of everything, staying ahead of everyone, has accelerated beyond anyone's control

In a world obsessed with mindless traffic in commercial goods, the products and profits, the sales and customers count— not we human beings.

Our way of life is not designed with real human interest in mind. Our way of life does not think of us humans at all. That's why we now have to begin to think of ourselves.

One thing is certain: freedom from our way of life will never be given to us by the system from the outside. Freedom from our way we must take for ourselves.

This is a very religious moment in the story of America's journey. We live in ethical times. We move through days that demand radical religious change. Only from God can we draw the strength to move out from under the economic empire we have built around ourselves, that has trapped us all under its nonnegotiable control.

With our backs to the wall we find ourselves back again where our Bible story begins. The holy story of the Jewish people making little bricks to build the enormous pyramids is the same holy story of our own conflict within our economic empire. They said to themselves as we must now say to ourselves, this misery causing way of life we live is not God's idea of what human life should be.

Monumental is the challenge facing every religious person today. As we face down the facts of our life situation, the need for the Exodus comes again. It is our turn for Exodus now.

When he came to Nazareth, where he had been brought up, he went to the synagogue on the sabbath day, as was his custom. He stood up to read, and the scroll of the prophet Isaiah was given to him. He unrolled the scroll and found the place where it was written:
"The Spirit of the Lord is upon me,
because he has anointed me
to bring good news to the poor.
He has sent me to proclaim release to the captives
and recovery of sight to the blind,
to let the oppressed go free,
to proclaim the year of the Lord's favor" (Luke 4:16–19).

Reinvent—
Another Word for Repent

Yet I have been the LORD your God
  ever since the land of Egypt;
you know no God but me,
  and besides me there is no savior.
It was I who fed you in the wilderness,
  in the land of drought.
When I fed them, they were satisfied;
  they were satisfied, and their heart was proud;
  therefore they forgot me (Hosea 13:4–6).

RELIGION BEGINS FOR ALL of us when we stop believing in our systems and begin to believe in the spirit of God active in our human souls.

When a way of life becomes so hurting to us that we can no longer believe in it, then as religious persons we are called upon to stand up and be counted as witnesses to an alternative lifestyle more faithful to the human race.

Moses was just another human being, like ourselves. Inside the social reality in which he found himself he saw his people wronged. He felt his people's pain. He sensed a call that came to him from the side of life not seen. A call he knew that *came from God*, a God who was always with his people. From vision to courage, from can do, to will do, taking life in his hands, he went for it. He made it the Exodus.

In the ongoing business of changing the course of human history, we Americans are now the ones called up to make difficult religious decisions.

Religion is our own response, to our own way of life, that is so destructive of us, and what *in God we are willing to do in our every bid to change it.*

When we think "religion" we are apt to think Bibles, buildings, institutions; let's think, rather, of individuals like Mahatma Gandhi, Nelson Mandela, Martin Luther King, Teresa of Calcutta. Religion is about human beings like ourselves who begin movements away from systems that are destructive of our humanity.

Our world changes only when the fearless few risk the risk and do what has never been done before. Rosa Parks, the black woman who sat up in the front of the bus in Montgomery, Alabama, and refused the back seat assigned her, sparked the civil rights movement and transformed America forever.

Every turnaround that has ever taken place in human history has begun inside a human soul. Freedom is never given. Freedom is taken by those with God-given guts who stand up against harmful opponents on the divine dignity of their own two God-given feet.

> *"Enter through the narrow gate; for the gate is wide and the road is easy that leads to destruction, and there are many who take it. For the gate is narrow and the road is hard that leads to life, and there are few who find it"* (Matthew 7:13–14).

Life Is Fearsome Stuff!

For what other great nation has a god so near to it as the LORD our God is whenever we call to him?
(Deuteronomy 4:7).

FEAR IS THE MOTOR force that undermines our best attempt at courage. In the days of Nazism there were many who did not agree with the Nazi system. In the days of Communism there were many who did not approve the Communist regime. Yet their fears muted their voices and melted them down into a silent compliance.

To realize how much our fears have power over us, all we have to do is to think back to our own childhood. Way back then, think about how much we feared even our parents in words we innocently expressed so many times to our friends: "My parents will kill me if I do this" or "I'm dead if they find out I did that."

It's shocking, when you think about it, that we couched the feelings we had and expressed from even our parents, whom we supposedly loved, in death threats. But it's a dynamic that worked both ways. Our parents, too, counted on our fears to keep us from cutting up too much or acting out of line.

As we grow up we do not grow out of these primal emotional states. We just transfer our fears to the persons we make big in our world today. They are the big mamas and the big papas who we feel we depend upon for our survival, whether it is true or not.

Those who have power over us today, those we make big— usually our bosses—replace our fathers and our mothers in our ordinary, everyday world. To them we give life-and-death control over our existence. They have the power to draw us back again into our childhood fears. With them aren't we in fact reduced to feeling like a little kid again?

Our fears keep us acting small; we say "Yes," instead of "No" to fit into the systems we now find ourselves in. Our fears keep us from standing on our own two feet. Our fears determine how we meet our world. Our fears decide how we live. We speak a lot about pressure and stress these days, but let's be honest when we speak of pressure and stress, what we are talking about is fear.

No one could pressure us; no one could stress us unless we were afraid of them. What are we saying when we say on the job, "I have to get this work done today or I am dead"? We are saying again what we said as kids. Our survival is tied to whatever situation we find ourselves in.

We adapt to our American reality by continuing playing small, doing things we don't want to do, going places we don't want to go, being with people we hate to be with—all because our fears keep us from just saying "No!"

We let the air out of our American pride once we acknowledge to ourselves that our fears, not our genius, conspire to create our frenetic way of life. Hurry, hurry, hurry, goes everyone scurrying all around us. Zoom, zoom, zoom, goes everyone everywhere passing us. We don't need a psychiatrist to tell us that our fears not our fun have set fire to our wheels.

Yet our fears are no excuse for remaining locked into a mode of living that is taking us all in the wrong direction.

Victims afraid of their freedom are not the saints of our Bible. No small courage do we associate with the stories of our great ones, Abraham, David, and Moses—all human beings of hair and skin, muscle and blood, just like ourselves. All of whom found their strength to stand up to the life situations in which they found themselves from the courage they received from their God within.

As religious persons, we too must rise above our fears and hold ourselves responsible for the economic empire of profitability and productivity we have built around us that values only products and profit and renders human beings insignificant.

Making our religion work for us, we understand this world that we take for granted; we take it apart; we move out from under its domination and overcome our enslavement to it.

The good news is that God so loved our world that to our world God sent God's only Son as one of our very own. In the most religious moment of our human story, Jesus proposed trust in God, not fear of our systems, as a new organizing center around which we could organize our world and recover the better side of our human nature.

"Do not fear those who kill the body but cannot kill the soul; rather fear him who can destroy both soul and body in hell. Are not two sparrows sold for a penny? Yet not one of them will fall to the ground apart from your Father. And even the hairs of your head are all counted. So do not be afraid; you are of more value than many sparrows" (Matthew 10:28–31).

Only Trust Matters

Blessed are those who trust in the LORD,
*   whose trust is the LORD.*
They shall be like a tree planted by water,
*   sending out its roots by the stream.*
It shall not fear when heat comes,
*   and its leaves shall stay green;*
in the year of drought it is not anxious,
*   and it does not cease to bear fruit* (Jeremiah 17:7–8)

WE MUST NEVER forget what kind of world it was that Jesus was born into—his world was not that much different from our own. In his day as in ours, society was not concerned primarily about human beings, so then as now living was controlled by fears.

Jesus was born into a fear-based culture, born in a land ruled by the Roman empire. Jesus grew up under an omnipresent, omnipowerful Roman presence that predetermined everyone's existence everywhere, keeping everyone in line. Rage and resentment circulated unforgivingly in a people beaten down by an all-controlling system.

Jesus was not the one to ignore what went on in his neighborhood. Jesus felt his people's pain. Jesus knew too well the maddening fears that melted them down and kept them caged in their daily prisons of servitude and subservience.

Jesus led his people to see how different their life could be if they could give up their fears of survival and make love of God and love of neighbor their first law of life. The centerpiece of Jesus' mission for our human transformation was the grassroots gathering of his people around supper tables, dinner tables, wherever they met at meals, relaxed at ease with one another, told stories, and talked life.

They brought with them their surplus foods, their grain and grapes, their fish and their wine to share with others. They took home with them what they needed from what others had shared with them.

In the giving and sharing of their resources, the followers of Jesus began to experience a new abundance. Everyone had plenty. All were givers. All were receivers. All were the richer for their mutual reciprocity.

Jesus knew that nothing in human history ever changes until people change themselves. So "repent," he said to them, meaning "Reinvent the way you feel, the way you believe, the way you behave within your world."

And so his followers moved away from their self-promoting, self-protecting ways. They began living off one another so they could live for each other.

Radical sharing replaced radical hoarding!
Radical hospitality replaced radical possessiveness!
All-forgiving love replaced unforgiving competition!

Jesus' followers transferred their energies away from fear of their world to care and concern for one another, making everyone else's needs their own. The hungry were given food. Strangers off the road were taken home. Nothing was lacking to anyone where everyone was inclined toward giving. It was the beginning of a new economy, the economy of love. Jesus named it the "Kingdom of God."

With fear at a minimum, and with trust at a maximum, a rival way of existing as human beings came to be. People's survival no longer depended on the Roman system. Jesus offered his people united in a supporting community of human service to one another this ingenious alternative lifestyle—and he still offers it to our world.

Jesus changed the way his people lived. The change he affected in the world he dwelt in we find recorded in the Acts of the Apostles:

> *Now the whole group of those who believed were of one heart and soul, and no one claimed private ownership of any possessions, but everything they owned was held in common. . . . There was not a needy person among them, for as many as owned lands or houses sold them and brought the proceeds of what was sold. They laid it at the apostles' feet, and it was distributed to each as any had need* (Acts 4:32, 34-35).

God's message in Jesus to us in America is clear: the functioning of our human society need not be based on survival fears. Our life can be lived another way if we move from our pride of possessing to the joy of sharing all that we own in holy caring for one another. But this requires repentance; this requires a fundamental change in our acquisitive habits of buying, getting, owning, and having things that in turn organize and govern the workings of our everyday world.

As possessions are made secondary to Jesus' way of living, only then will we become givers instead of takers; only then will our attitude be generosity not storage, our mindset hospitality not competition. Following Jesus we will create an environment making everyone feel welcome.

We will think differently of persons.
We will see persons differently.
We will be with persons in a totally different way
than the way we are with one another every day now.

Putting persons back where persons belong, at the heart of all that we are, we will create a world of talking and listening, a world of receiving and giving, where our true personal connection to one another matters more than anything else in our world.

"Do not be afraid, little flock, for it is your Father's good pleasure to give you the kingdom. Sell your possessions, and give alms. Make purses for yourselves that do not wear out, an unfailing treasure in heaven, where no thief comes near and no moth destroys. For where your treasure is, there your heart will be also" (Luke 12:32–34).

The World Before Christ...
The World After

. . . you will seek the LORD your God, and you will find him
if you search after him with all your heart and soul.
In your distress, when all these things have happened to you
in time to come, you will return to the LORD your God and
heed him. Because the LORD your God is a merciful god,
he will neither abandon you nor destroy you; he will not
forget the covenant with your ancestors that he swore to
them (Deuteronomy 4:29–31).

HUMAN HISTORY IS NOW a divided highway marked by
time, the time recorded before Jesus and the time after marked
by his coming. In Jesus God placed human beings above systems,
above institutions. In Jesus God put human beings back where
they belong at the center of the human world. In Jesus God
placed us in the care of one another. In Jesus we ask ourselves as
Americans, If we are not living for each other now, then what are
we living for?

No small matter to Jesus is the issue of our human possessions and what to do with them. Resolute in his own lifestyle to
be free from possessions, he asks as much of all his followers.

Freed from their nets and their boats and their properties, Jesus freed the early disciples to be there for one another in hospitable, generous ways.

Jesus is religion made simple. People always come first. Material goods are always secondary to the welfare of human beings. When the final curtain falls and the human show on earth is over our final report card will be based not on what we own, but on what we gave away to those more needy than ourselves.

Hopefully we will hear Jesus say to us as in the gospel of Matthew (25): "Come. You have my Father's blessing! Inherit the kingdom prepared for you from the creation of the world. For I was hungry and you gave me food, I was thirsty and you gave me drink. I was a stranger and you welcomed me, naked and you clothed me, in prison and you came to visit me. I assure you, as often as you did it for one of my least ones, you did it for me."

In Jesus God has made our human needs his very own. In Jesus God asks us all to do the same. We are all called to a lifetime of making sure everyone on this earth has enough.

It is amazing how well we know every word that Jesus spoke. It is equally amazing how we ignore everything Jesus asked us to do. We have kept the words; but we have lost the passion Jesus felt for human beings. Our way of life does not compute with his at all; if anything, we Americans demonstrate the polar opposite of his lifestyle.

The world order by which we arrange our existence from day to day is merciless at the core to other human persons. The insidious accentuation on excessive production and marketing of needless products steals attention away from our human needs. Any meaningful interpersonal connection to one another gets sacrificed to our workaholic, shopaholic, lifestyles.

The logic of our commercial system is extravagance in excess. So whoever lives the system must keep pace with its wanton wastefulness; human beings be damned. We Americans have totally missed or purposely ignored Jesus' frugal style of living, his voluntary poverty, his penny-pinching simplicity that made his life so festive in a banquet of plenty where everyone had their necessities for living because everyone was given to giving.

It was a stingy way of surviving barely, where persons could be dependent on others as others were dependent on them. The revolutionary option God offers humanity in Jesus is to live on love, to live by love, to live for love. We Americans think such a proposal is totally impractical.

Yet as religious persons we can no longer run, duck, hide, or avoid the fact that for now and for evermore humanity has been touched by a moment in human history when God in Jesus put us in the care of one another, and asked us to make everyone else's cause our own. Technology and the advantages of our times have made us realize that the earth is our living room, our home, our address. Every human being on earth is family to us. We are all related in God's space-shuttle earth. We are all God's kids.

From an ethical standpoint as religious persons we can no longer in conscience subordinate everyone else in order to pamper ourselves stockpiling our perks while our brothers and sisters are squeezed out of the basics they need to survive.

Whatever the justification we may give for a market economy, it can no longer be business as usual. We can no longer say to ourselves that what I do with my life is nobody's business but my own. We know that everything we do, everything we are, affects every other passenger on this little spacecraft we call earth.

Nor can we any longer piggyback on Jesus declaring Jesus to be our personal Savior, all the while covering our assets and gaining our profits, going to church on Sunday and back to the commercial fields on Monday, hoping to make a killing, and seeing no contradiction between our religion and the bloated way we live.

The possibility of living otherwise than we live now is not an impossible religious calling. It means struggling out of the straightjacket we have tied ourselves into. It means for all of us shifting the focus of our lives from things back to persons, from money back to human beings. Our recovery is the rediscovering of persons and human relationships as the centerpiece of our human existence.

As Americans behaving badly, what we have done wrong is that we have failed to remember what Jesus reminds us of, that life is not about possessions, life is about persons; life is about love.

We Americans are people who love. Love is the reason we good people live every day. We love but our love is small. Our love is limited to family, relatives, and friends. In Jesus God is asking for more.

Jesus, looking at him, loved him and said, "You lack one thing; go, sell what you own, and give the money to the poor, and you will have treasure in heaven; then come follow me." When he heard this, he was shocked and went away grieving, for he had many possessions (Mark 10:21–22).

Too Many Fans, Not Enough Followers

> *. . . for my people have committed two evils:*
> *they have forsaken me,*
> *the fountain of living water,*
> *and dug out cisterns for themselves,*
> *cracked cisterns*
> *that can hold no water* (Jeremiah 2:13).

IN THE GLARE of history, forever he stands the Jesus of Israel, the Christ of the Christians, a tragic figure who belongs to the ages, a signpost pointing to another way we human beings could be living with one another. Our world is unthinkable without him. And yet our world today goes on as if he never existed.

We human beings have regressed again to the way we were before he came. Human life today is still not about human beings. In our time as in his time human beings are exploitable, expendable, disposable, and dispensable.

In a market economy where we turn unnecessary products into absolute necessities, we reduce human beings from our first priority; human beings always come second to money. Our aggressive, assertive, competitive, predatory world is further

away from valuing human beings today than it was in the days of
Jesus Christ.

Jesus still draws a crowd. People still go wild over Jesus. So
famous is Jesus now that no one pays attention to his vision
anymore. We read and read the gospels so often that after a
while the words lose their meaning—they all begin to sound like
"Have a nice day!"

Long, long ago the way of Jesus lost its edge, its oddness, its
deeper kind of living, its deeper kind of loving that involves a
deeper kind of relational existence. The prospect of an alternative humanity is still the offering Jesus puts forward to us. But to
give love, to receive love according to the standard established by
Jesus, we must undergo a foundational change, a transformation
of a deeply religious nature.

*Then [Jesus] told them a parable: "The land of a rich man
produced abundantly. And he thought to himself, 'What
should I do, for I have no place to store my crops?' Then he
said, 'I will do this: I will pull down my barns and build
larger ones, and there I will store all my grain and my
goods. And I will say to my soul, 'Soul, you have ample
goods laid up for many years; relax, eat, drink, be merry.'
But God said to him, 'You fool! This very night your life is
being demanded of you. And the things you have prepared,
whose will they be?' So it is with those who store up
treasures for themselves but are not rich toward God"*
(Luke 12:16–21).

Jesus Is So Un-American

Even though you offer me your burnt offerings
and grain offerings,
I will not accept them;
and the offerings of well-being of your fatted animals
I will not look upon.
Take away from me the noise of your songs;
I will not listen to the melody of your harps.
But let justice roll down the waters,
and righteousness like an ever-flowing stream
(Amos 5:22–24).

WE AMERICANS ARE by nature a very religious people. We have churches, temples, synagogues—almost one on every corner. God has been good to us. Religion comes easy to us. The pews are comfortable under our behinds. In the holy halls where we come to pray, it is "God Bless America" that we come to sing.

The assumption underlying our holy gathering is that we are living in God's own country. America is the best of the best, the greatest nation ever, and we ourselves, of course, are God's dream of human beings come true.

Patriotism and worship, flag and Bible, hang together in our holy places. One hand washes the other. Sunday service is easy listening—just sticking our nose inside God's door, nothing threatening, nothing much, just staying in touch. Life is comfy in our religious worship.

Our religion is a step back in time. Our preference is for the past. Our religion tells it like it was, not how it is. We wax eloquent about God in our sacred texts, God in our sacred traditions but it is God as God was we are into, not God as God is now, in the spiritual flatness of weekends spent in shopping malls, searching for life's deepest meanings in filled-up shopping bags, in loaded-up shopping carts. Religion ignores and does not speak to our consuming consumer madness, that puts us down, and keeps us down, in an underworld of economic slavery.

What if on the Sabbath or on the Sunday we were to go to our places of worship and there the preacher exploded in a tirade of honesty, shoved the knife of God straight into the heart of our mad, awful greed, saying to us in a manner reminiscent of the prophets of old:

> *God forgives us Yanks,*
> *   spoiled brats of creation.*
> *To gratify our insatiable habits*
> *   of compulsive shopping,*
> *   we have blocked off for ourselves a patch of plenty*
> *   in a planet of human misery.*
> *Keeping for ourselves what we have too much of,*
> *   we keep the rest of the world from getting*
> *   what they need to survive.*
> *The slow dying each day of millions*
> *   of human beings from malnutrition,*
> *that's what feeds ice cream to our faces.*

Our eyes are bigger than our bellies.
Taking human bites from the loaf of life
cannot satisfy our ferocious appetite
to have it all.

In mad excess, almost animal in our drives,
we tear off, we rip up,
we waste, we throw away.
We want everything.
We have no sense of anything.
We are 4 percent of the earth's population;
we consume 40 percent of the earth's resources.
Everything magnificent in the natural world
we have turned into trash for our dumpster.

To fill our needs we pollute the skies
and deplete the earth.
We dim the sun by day with smog.
At night our smoke blacks out the stars.
We pour chemicals into our fields,
pesticides into our foods.
We make a waste way of our waterways.
Our oceans are sewerage systems.
Our beaches are backed up toilet bowls.
Fighting time the biosphere is dying
the death of our good earth is drawing near.
God's palms are sweating now;
God's earth is not forever.
The biggest problem facing God today
is that we, God's children, are destroying God's earth.
And God can't do a thing to stop us
because God has made us free.

Taking the Time to Love

How free are we?
This free we are!
Free to ransack and destroy
the living room of life.
Free to rip off the system,
screw up the process
and not give a damn for anything or anyone
as long as we can get what we want out of life.

Every day the rising sun meets the big sky over America.
And there we are down below,
bulldozing marshlands into shopping malls,
grasslands into highways,
wildernesses into developments.
The reach and range of what we need
in order to be happy is frightening.

What is it we lack?
What is it we are looking for?
What is it we have such a great need of?
What is it that fiercely compels our consumer compulsions?
Why do we need such a surfeit of everything?

In our endless, mindless, relentless
traffic in commercial goods,
we are all doing irreparable damage
to the earth's resources
by our nonsustainable lifestyle.

We have no future for ourselves,
nor for our children.
Neither has the human race.
The lifetime of life on the planet earth

*will soon be over just because of us
    in our self-destructive drive.
We are taking everyone else
    out with us in our suicidal mischief.*

*From the ethical standpoint
    of any of our world religions,
    our extravagance in abundance
    is morally scandalous.*

*But there is no stopping us now.
It is all we have to live for.
We'll kill and we'll die
    And we'll go to war for "the American way of life."
It is not easy to know how to reach us.
Our needs are terrifying.
Truth never gets past our defenses.
We are indeed a World Power.
But our power is not of the human heart,
    nor is it of the human spirit.
Our power is bully power
    that comes from our sophisticated weapons
    that could in seconds vaporize the planet.*

*How like the Roman empire
    we are in the manner of our ways.
How much terror we employ
    to maintain our way of life.
Petrified are we that we won't get it all.
Fearful are we that we should lose
    all of what we have got.
We are not so innocent
    as to not know what we are doing.*

Taking the Time to Love

We keep the poor, poor
so we can keep what we have got,
even though we have right now at our fingertips
the wherewithal for their deliverance
from world hunger.

Too well we know, ours is not an infinite earth,
but nonetheless a planet with enough for everyone,
if we Americans were only willing
to pass around our Eucharist.
But our capacity to share
and our ability to feel for other human beings
is far less than our unforgiving drive to have it all.

Spanning the ages of human history,
graves of millions of humans
down billions of years
Lie under the emergence of our nation as a people.
Surely be to God,
it was not to make money
and to buy up the world
that God brought our nation to birth.
No, but as Jesus has shown us,
God brought us here
to make life and to make love
for ourselves and for one another.
God's wish for our world
made manifest in Jesus
is a communal world,
where all humans have equal access
to a pantry of goods
where God has supplied a plenty for all.

Our call as Americans
is to share the abundance
by beginning to live simply
so that others may simply live.

"Not everyone who says to me, 'Lord, Lord,' will enter
the kingdom of heaven, but only the one who does the will
of my Father in heaven. On that day many will say to me,
'Lord, Lord, did we not prophesy in your name, and do
many deeds of power in your name?' Then I will declare to
them, 'I never knew you; go away from me, you evildoers'"
(Matthew 7:21–23).

We Are What We Own

When Israel was a child, I loved him,
*   and out of Egypt I called my son.*
The more I called them,
*   the more they went from me;*
They kept sacrificing to the Baals,
*   and offering incense to idols.*
Yet it was I who taught Ephraim to walk,
*   I took them up in my arms;*
*   but they did not know that I healed them.*
I led them with cords of human kindness,
*   with bands of love.*
*   I was to them like those*
*   who lift infants to their cheeks.*
*   I bent down to them and fed them. . . .*
My heart recoils within me;
*   my compassion grows warm and tender.*
I will not execute my fierce anger;
*   I will not again destroy Ephraim;*
for I am God and no mortal,
*   the Holy One in your midst,*
*   and I will not come in wrath* (Hosea 11:1–4, 8–9).

TOUGH LOVE, TOUGH TALK, tough religion may force us all to look at America from a more critical point of view. But we must be kind and deeply compassionate with ourselves because our fears make us live the way we do, not our maliciousness.

America is the arrangement of reality we poor humans have devised to organize ourselves against the chaos that daily threatens our human existence.

It is our tried and true mode of self-preservation, even if our setup boxes us again and again into an economic corner. It still is the only way we know how to control our vulnerable, fragile, precarious, human predicament.

Granted, there is desperation in the way life is lived in America, but there is desperation everywhere all across the planet where humans struggle to survive in a world that is so inhospitable to our basic human needs of water, clothing, food, and shelter.

America offers us a plan of total coverage, how we are to meet our world. We live under the umbrella of its guaranteed protection. Issues of survival, security, prestige, social standing, peer approval, all the powerful stuff that shapes and determines our human identity are taken care of by our habits of living America style.

Soul and body we are American. America lives in us. We live in it. There is a oneness without difference between us and America. Like fish in water we are inseparable from it. This is why in our most honest-to-God moments we must acknowledge that the bonds that bind us to America have more to do with symbiotic terrors of self-preservation than the glitzy freedom of liberated persons we project to the world.

Ours is an inherited way of doing life. Those who came before us brought us to this moment in our history. We are not to blame for where we are, but as religious persons we find ourselves living on the wrong side of the Bible. The accepted cliché that greed is good puts us on the bad side of God.

America is still a very young nation. Our story is so like the young man in the gospel who came to Jesus saying, *"Teacher, what good deed must I do to have eternal life?"*

Jesus told him: *"If you wish to be perfect, go, sell your possessions, and give the money to the poor, and you will have treasure in heaven; then come, follow me." When the young man heard this word, he went away grieving, for he had many possessions* (Matthew 19:21–22).

His self-esteem was tied to the self-importance of what was his. Like ourselves, he was owned by the ownership of what he owned. All Jesus asked of him is what Jesus asks of us, to divest ourselves of material things so we can reinvest ourselves in human beings.

"Jerusalem, Jerusalem, the city that kills the prophets and stones those who are sent to it! How often have I desired to gather your children together as a hen gathers her brood under her wings, and you were not willing! See your house is left to you. And I tell you, you will not see me until the time comes when you say, 'Blessed is the one who comes in the name of the Lord' " (Luke 13:34–35).

God Loves the Underdog

Woe to him who builds his house by unrighteousness
  and his upper rooms by injustice;
who makes his neighbors work for nothing,
  and does not give them their wages;
who says, "I will build myself a spacious house
  with large upper rooms,"
and who cuts out windows for it,
  paneling it with cedar,
  and painting it with vermilion.
Are you a king
  because you compete in cedar?
Did not your father eat and drink
  and do justice and righteousness?
  Then it was well with him.
He judged the cause of the poor and needy;
  then it was well.
Is not this to know me?
  says the Lord.
But your eyes and heart
  are only on your dishonest gain,
for shedding innocent blood,
  and for practicing oppression and violence
(Jeremiah 22:13–17).

GOD SO LOVES US human beings that God has always intervened in our human affairs to keep on the straight and narrow way of attending to each others needs, making others' needs our own.

The Bible is the diary we humans have kept with our God. Page after page it is unmistakably clear what God is on to, what God is into, in speaking to us through the prophets. Through God's prophets God pleads with us to stop taking advantage of others. God begs us to stop squeezing others out of what they need to survive in order to satisfy our own oversized greed.

> *Hear this, you that trample on the needy*
> *and bring to ruin the poor of the land,*
> *saying, "When will the new moon be over*
> *so that we may sell our grain,*
> *and the Sabbath,*
> *so that we may offer wheat for sale?*
> *We will make the ephah small, and the shekel great,*
> *and practice deceit with false balances,*
> *buying the poor for silver*
> *and the needy for a pair of sandals,*
> *and selling the sweepings of the wheat"* (Amos 8:4–11).

Times will keep on changing as this old world keeps on turning, but the command of love that we love one another as God loves us will always be the same.

The message of the Bible is always very simple, always very plain in our ordinary, everyday world. God begs us to stop foraging, stop hoarding, stop storing, stop stockpiling properties and possessions in a manner that cheats others out of their basic needs.

> *"Alas for you who heap up what is not your own!"*
> *How long will you load yourselves with goods taken in pledge?*

"Alas for you who get evil gain for your houses,
  setting your nest on high
  to be safe from the reach of harm!" (Habakkuk 2:6, 9)

God felt so strong about the impulse of our human greed and its potential harm to us that God made it the tenth commandment of the Decalogue. *"Thou shalt not covet thy neighbor's goods."*

There is nothing extraterrestrial about our Bible at all. It is as down home as loving parents talking to their kids, asking them to stop fighting with one another, begging them to stop hurting each other, and pleading with them to share their toys and their things with one another.

God's love for us, God's kids, is such that God gets angry with our greed. Wanting always more than we need we deprive others of what they need to survive.

Alas for those who devise wickedness
  and evil deeds on their beds!
When the morning dawns, they perform it,
  because it is in their power.
They covet fields, and seize them;
  houses, and take them away;
they oppress householder and house,
  people and their inheritance (Micah 2:1–2).

We Americans are a Bible proud people, proud of the Bible's influences and background in the birth of our nation. We all know from our Bible that what we own we owe to God. We cannot know our Bible and not know that what we own God wishes us to share with others.

And the crowds asked [John the Baptist], "What then should we do?" In reply he said to them, "Whoever has two coats must share with anyone who has none; and whoever has food must do likewise." Even tax collectors came to be baptized, and they asked him, "Teacher, what should we do?" He said to them, "Collect no more than the amount prescribed for you." Soldiers also asked him, "And we, what should we do?" He said to them, "Do not extort money from anyone by threats or false accusation, and be satisfied with your wages" (Luke 3:10–14).

God's desperate wish to get us humans to share all we have with one another took a mind-blowing turn when God's only Son became one of our very own.

Long ago God spoke to our ancestors in many and various ways by the prophets, but in these last days, he has spoken to us by a Son, whom he appointed heir of all things, through whom he also created the worlds (Hebrews 1:1–2).

What is God in Jesus doing in our world except saying to us:

And [Jesus] said to them, "Take care! Be on your guard against all kinds of greed; for one's life does not consist in the abundance of possessions. Then he told them a parable: "The land of a rich man produced abundantly. And he thought to himself, 'What should I do, for I have no place to store my crops?' Then he said, 'I will do this: I will pull down my barns and build larger ones, and there I will store all my grain and all my goods. And I will say to my soul, 'Soul, you have ample goods laid up for many years; relax, eat, drink, be merry.' But God said to him, 'You fool! This very night your life is being demanded of you. And the things you have prepared, whose will they be?' So it is with those who store up treasures for themselves but are not rich toward God" (Luke 12:15–21).

We Americans ignore God's Bible, ignore God's prophets, and even ignore what God in Jesus has told us—we have done the very opposite. We have created an award-winning, top-honored enterprise of attaining, acquiring, owning, and possessing material goods. We have made a virtue of expanding, extending, and monopolizing our holdings. We heap praise on ourselves in the admirable enterprise of scavenging everything, everywhere, from everyone all around the world.

We have done it all, of course, in the name of business. All is done in evenhanded legality because greed now is good and coveting our neighbor's goods is no longer considered wrong. The tenth commandment is long gone; it disappeared down the long forgotten highway of our precommercial, preindustrial days.

No one hesitates a moment to notice or to wonder what all this means to human beings and what all this is doing to ourselves. As God always knew and as we will all find out sooner or later, when life is all about possessions and not about persons, life never gets better—life always gets worse.

In practical terms, what is Jesus' project for us Americans except that we stop amassing wealth, that we cease increasing our belongings, so that we no longer need storage space to house our hoardings. Instead, God in Jesus calls us to see the magnificence of persons as contrasted to the advertised magnificence of manu-factured products.

Following Jesus means putting persons first, front and center, in every way we approach existence. What this entails is nothing less than one almighty conversion for us all, as we move from being addicted consumers of material goods and services to becoming persons who attend to each other, who minister to each person by giving of our fullest presence as modeled for us in the person of Jesus.

So Jesus called them and said to them, "You know that among the Gentiles those whom they recognize as their rulers lord it over them, and their great ones are tyrants over them. But it is not so among you; but whoever wishes to become great among you must be your servant, and whoever wishes to be first among you must be slave of all. For the Son of Man came not to be served but to serve, and to give his life a ransom for many" (Mark 10:42–45).

Every Human Being Matters

If there is among you anyone in need, a member of your community in any of your towns within the land that the LORD your God is giving you, do not be hard-hearted or tight-fisted toward your needy neighbor. You should rather open your hand, willingly lending enough to meet the need, whatever it may be (Deuteronomy 15:7–8).

NO ONE KNOWS Jesus without also knowing that Jesus was the one who offered love to everyone. Jesus went out into the highways and byways to be there for those who had cast life aside. The shamed, the belittled, the neglected, those not worthy of anybody's time—for them Jesus was there.

Down and dirty in our down-and-dirty world, Jesus had friends in low places. Jesus privileged those who struggle from below. Jesus was at home with the sorriest of souls. A world that trivializes human persons came to see through Jesus' eyes a world where every human being matters to God.

Jesus ate and drank with the worst of them. Those who would never be accepted, never belong, never be respected by respectable people, Jesus respected. The God-wide heart of Jesus *embraced them all.*

Jesus saw no bad in anyone. Jesus saw a side to human beings no one ever saw before. And few have seen ever since. Jesus saw in human beings something we still have to see in ourselves. Jesus saw only the good.

The love that pumped through the heart of Jesus was God-force, the uncompromising love of human beings. Jesus adored the human race. And in his own manner Jesus asked us to reevaluate how we value human beings.

> *"When you give a luncheon or a dinner, do not invite your friends or your brothers or your relatives or rich neighbors, in case they may invite you in return, and you would be repaid. But when you give a banquet, invite the poor, the crippled, the lame, and the blind. And you will be blessed, because they cannot repay you, for you will be repaid at the resurrection of the righteous"* (Luke 14:12–14).

We have no need to ask what God in Jesus asks us to care about. Jesus' daily practice put the spotlight on the priority of every single person. He beckons us to do the same.

> *Then Jesus went about all the cities and villages, teaching in their synagogues, and proclaiming the good news of the kingdom, and curing every disease and every sickness. When he saw the crowds, he had compassion for them, because they were harassed and helpless, like sheep without a shepherd. Then he said to his disciples, "The harvest is plentiful, but the laborers are few; therefore ask the Lord of the harvest to send out laborers into his harvest"* (Matthew 9:35–37).

The Status We Give
Our Professions

Let the same mind be in you that was in Christ Jesus,
who, though he was in the form of God,
did not regard equality with God
as something to be exploited,
but emptied himself,
taking the form of a slave,
being born in human likeness.
And being found in human form,
he humbled himself
and became obedient to the point of death—
even death on a cross (Philippians 2:5–8).

WHAT WE NOTICE most is that the socially powerful values that power our existence are those that emphasize technologies, commodities, properties, development, investments, real estate. The focus of our interest always tends to be in a nonpersonal area. The dominant occupations, the ones that carry the most prestige are those that bring home the money.

The flip side of looking up to certain occupations as big time is that we look down on other occupations as small time. We look down on people and consider them who take care of people second rate. The workers who care for our children in daycare centers, the staff workers who care for our parents in senior care centers, the school bus drivers who drive our children to school are all made to feel that they are holding down lesser jobs, and so they are given lesser pay.

Teachers, social workers, counselors at drug care centers—all the occupations that give nurture to others—we rate, we rank, we grade as second-rate jobs performed by lesser persons who are paid less, and sometimes not paid at all.

Life-giving, life-nourishing and life-enhancing activities such as those done by mothers are seen as a lesser calling. Even what the mothers of our children do, we write off as "kids' stuff"— meeting the school bus after school, walking a child home along the road, baking a birthday cake, having her child's friends over to celebrate, washing clothes, cleaning house, making a home a human place. According to our system of values, there is no status in doing these things. They are not noteworthy endeavors. They are all unworthy of our important person time.

Despite what Jesus has shown us by his lifestyle, we feel that just being there for each other in an on-going, always reliable way is an inferior way to live our days. It's the crime against humanity that we commit—we overvalue money property and possessions because we so undervalue human beings.

> *Then [Jesus] said to them all, "If any want to become my followers, let them deny themselves and take up their cross daily and follow me. For those who want to save their life will lose it, and those who lose their life for my sake will save it. What does it profit them if they gain the whole world, but lose or forfeit themselves?"* (Luke 9:23–25)

71

Living the Jesus Way

A new heart I will give you, and a new spirit I will put within you; and I will remove from your body the heart of stone and give you a heart of flesh. I will put my spirit within you, and make you follow my statutes and be careful to observe my ordinances. Then you shall live in the land that I gave to your ancestors; and you shall be my people, and I will be your God (Ezekiel 36:26–28).

AS RELIGIOUS PERSONS we are a conflicted people, split in our loyalties by false priorities. What has most meaning for us is our deep connection with each other. What has most value for us is our lifestyle.

Positions, possessions, property, money, school, work take up most of our time. There is where we place our emphasis. Our loved ones must make do with our left-over time.

We all say to ourselves, we say it to one another, if we were not so tied down with the demands of making ends meet we would all live like Mother Teresa.

There is a knowing in us that knows our being there for others is the reason God brought us here. For our contemporary world Mother Teresa is the cherished expression of our better self.

Stapled to our visual brain are those pictures of Mother Teresa bending down over street persons hugging them up in her arms and loving them back into life. Instinctively, intuitively, we all say to ourselves: That's what life is all about. Life is hugs! Life is love! Life is being there for others! Through Mother Teresa we learn that love can live again in any human heart as love was lived in the heart of Jesus Christ.

The love for other human beings that Jesus calls for is not from some other realm foreign to our own. It is here-on-earth love. Jesus comes back and lives again in any person of our own time who sees in other persons what he saw, who feels for others what he felt.

What if this same passion for human beings that drove Jesus to his crucifixion were to take over us so totally that, like Mother Teresa, we became totally changed in the way we reached out to one another?

The motivation and inspiration for such a transformation can come to us from no less a person than Jesus Christ himself who, like ourselves, was tempted in every way but never sinned. We ought to be grateful to the gospel writers who had the courage to write into the story of Jesus the episode of his temptations in the desert, because his struggles were so much like our own.

What are we to make of the urges inside Jesus that so bugged him to throw himself off the temple top, or to change stones into bread? It was the devil's plea within him to display his abilities for the world to see and so make himself important with the people of his time. This is what the showdown in the desert was all about.

This is the same old showdown that goes on each day in our own inner hearts. We, too, are all torn up inside between the drive that urges us to become somebody big in the eyes of others in the world out there, and the drive that urges us to live a life of service like Mother Teresa, catering to the vulnerable needs of those around us.

There in the wilderness, in the heart of human darkness, Jesus made the decisions that made him Jesus. After that, in a makeshift life he spent his days breaking bread, sharing wine, celebrating simple human company with simple human beings.

No hurry in his head, lazy and easy was his style, emptied out of his own importance, he had room and he had time for everyone he met along the way. In the role of "best friend" he set about saving the world. Jesus just hung out with those whose life had burned out, an insider inside each one's journey so they could feel with him the love God had for them.

The final gesture of Jesus' unstinting brand of loving and living for others was enacted for our world, to be emulated by us all, on the night before he died:

> *Jesus knew that his hour had come to depart from this world and go to the Father. Having loved his own who were in the world, he loved them to the end. . . . [Jesus] got up from the table, took off his outer robe, and tied a towel around himself. Then he poured water into a basin and began to wash the disciples' feet and to wipe them with the towel that was tied around him. . . . After he had washed their feet, had put on his robe, and had returned to the table, he said to them, "Do you know what I have done to you? You call me Teacher and Lord—and you are right, for that is what I am. So if I, your Lord and Teacher, have washed your feet, you also ought to wash one another's feet. For I have set you an example, that you also should do as I have done to you* (John 13:1–15).

Jesus is an event of earth and time that calls us to be more human, human beings, in the "Jesus way" we live, simply following his example by being there for one another in our ordinary everyday world.

Beloved, let us love one another, because love is from God; everyone who loves is born of God and knows God. Whoever does not love does not know God, for God is love (1 John 4:7–8).

We Discover Ourselves in Jesus

Am I a God near by, says the LORD, and not a God far off?
Who can hide in secret places so that I cannot see them? says
the LORD. Do I not fill heaven and earth? Says the LORD
(Jeremiah 23:23–24).

THERE IS SOMETHING in us as human beings that discovers something of ourselves in Jesus. He is in us; we are in him. We are each other. Our souls connect. Jesus calls out to the Jesus in us. There is in every human being the potential of becoming another Jesus. Jesus became what we are so that we might become what he is.

We poor human beings who are being blown sideways through life find our compass in Jesus. When asked by life itself who we are and what our lives mean to us, it is to Jesus that we point. It is his kind of life we would love to live. The self we live with, the self each one of us is, sees our own true self lived out in Jesus. Jesus calls out to the Jesus in us.

Like ourselves, Jesus had one shot at life.

Like ourselves, Jesus had to ask himself every day, How shall I live today?

Like ourselves, the life that was Jesus' life was what he did with life.

Like ourselves, who Jesus was and who he ultimately became was worked out in the personal center of his own inner soul.

Like ourselves, without grandeur, beset by setbacks, through drab, dull, wet, cold, ordinary days, Jesus played the hand that life had dealt him. He made do with what life gave him. He stood up to what life did to him.

Like ourselves, the spin he put into human life was done in the odd way—he moved through his own days.

Like ourselves, what Jesus was like Jesus showed by what he said and what he did in every situation in which he found himself.

Like ourselves, the life-long agony of Jesus, the making of his own soul, was done in how he moved of his own accord through actual, external, cultural, social situations of his time.

Like ourselves, his stance, his gestures, his style, his way of response told the outside world of his love of human beings that burned inside.

Like ourselves, Jesus went through life in the form of a story.

Like ourselves, when his story was over, his story was told by the decision he made to live the life he lived.

Jesus turned us down a road we humans now can take.

What Jesus was, he asked us to become.
What Jesus did, he asked us to do.
He was the love he asked us to live
He was the trust he asked us to be.
He was the humility he asked us to imitate.
He was the poverty he asked us to practice.
Jesus walked us through;
Jesus showed us how.
What Jesus did is doable;
It is our turn to do it now.

This is what Jesus means
When he says to each one of us,
Come, follow me!

Since, then, we have a great high priest who has passed through the heavens, Jesus, the Son of God, let us hold fast to our confession. For we do not have a high priest who is unable to sympathize with our weaknesses, but we have one who in every respect has been tested as we are, yet without sin (Hebrews 4:14–16).

Our Divine Connection

God's love was revealed among us in this way: God sent his only Son into the world so that we might live through him. In this is love, not that we loved God but that he loved us and sent his Son to be the atoning sacrifice for our sins. Beloved, since God loved us so much, we also ought to love one another (1 John 4:9–11).

A BETTER WORD for love is the word "connection." We can then translate God's double law of love into:

> *Thou shalt be connected*
>> *to the Lord Your God*
>> *with all your heart,*
>> *with all your soul,*
>> *with all your mind,*
>> *and with all your strength.*
> *And you shall be connected*
>> *with your neighbor*
>> *as you are connected to yourself.*

When we describe religion as our divine connection with God and our human connection with one another, this is the sense of connection we all experience for ourselves in our houses of worship.

In the holy houses where we gather to pray, feelings of relatedness well up inside us. At silent times we join our hands and bow our heads in prayer. Close to our own feelings we feel close to the feelings of others.

Bondedness, belongingness, connectedness—this is what we experience when we congregate together in our communities of faith.

If we contrast the way we act in our churches, temples, and synagogues with the way we behave when we are in our cars driving out on our roadways, we discover that we live in two very opposite worlds. We discover that we are two very different persons in these two very different spaces.

The most honest reading we can ever get on ourselves and how we feel about other human beings who we do not know personally and who don't know us is the way we behave behind the wheel.

Waves and smiles are not the language of our roads. Read our lips. Swears curl up our surly faces. When we pass other drivers, they know it is not "God bless you" we are saying behind our windshield.

Inside the combat tanks of our cars, behind the wheel, it is "Get out of my way or I'll run you off the road." "You stupid S.O.B." Stopped at a light, lips clenched, the "drop dead" look at other drivers as we rev our engines to beat them out before the changing of the light, and then of course the middle finger for the open road—we couldn't drive without them.

Pity the poor soul whose car stalls in the thick of traffic. We honk our horn. Who the hell do they think they are blocking our personal highway.

Riding around in our armored cars we're in a homicidal state of mind. At church on Sunday we're some other person allowing people in and out before us, enabling them to get to their places.

Our church manners are the manners of Jesus; our road manners are the manners of our culture. Tailgating, lights flashing, self-involved in our tailor-tight schedules, pursuing our own earth-shaking projects, we treat other drivers as individuals of no significance, nonpersons. Not only are human beings secondary entities in our American way of life, they are also secondary in the mad express of our own agendas.

The way we drive is who we are. It is the American way, the way of disconnection. The way we are in church is the way we ought to be, the way to deep connection that Jesus opened for us.

Our human hearts cry out today for America's return to the warm, connected way of life profiled for us by Jesus. It is the world envisioned by Jesus that has gone into eclipse somewhere down our American years. It is the missing dimension in our aggressive, competitive, commercial razor-blade way of living.

The way of feeling and affection.
The way of reverence and respect.
The way of care and concern.
The way of sensitivity and cooperation.
The way of lovingness and connectedness.
The way of openness and relatedness.
The way of treating each other mutually as equals.
The way of living with others as relatives.
The way of sharing the earth in mutual cooperatives.
The way of surrendering to closeness, intimacy, and warmth.
The way of human connection marked by our honoring the divine nobility of every person.

The way of life mapped out for us by God in Jesus entails a lot of time, and we don't have that kind of time to be with people in a deep connected way anymore, except maybe on the Sabbath, or on Sundays.

"As the Father has loved me, so I have loved you; abide in my love. If you keep my commandments, you will abide in my love, just as I have kept my Father's commandments and abide in his love. I have said these things to you so that my joy may be in you, and that your joy may be complete (John 15:9–11).

What Is Time For?

For you were called to freedom, brothers and sisters; only do not use your freedom as an opportunity for self-indulgence, but through love become slaves to one another. For the whole law is summed up in a single commandment, "You shall love your neighbor as yourself." . . .
Live by the Spirit, I say, and do not gratify the desires of the flesh. . . .
By contrast, the fruit of the Spirit is love, joy, peace, patience, kindness, generosity, faithfulness, gentleness, and self-control. There is no law against such things. And those who belong to Christ Jesus have crucified the flesh with its passions and desires. If we live by the Spirit, let us also be guided by the Spirit (Galatians 5:13–14, 16, 22–25).

WHEN SOMEONE SAYS to you they don't have time, they are saying I don't have time for what you want me to have time for. Or even deeper than that, they are saying I don't have time for you. The excuse of having no time, if truth be told, is no excuse at all. Because we all have time for what we want to have time for!

Golfers have time for golf. Swimmers have time for swimming. Rock climbers have time for climbing rocks. Gamblers have time for gambling. We all do our thing and we all make sure we make the time to do it.

The pope does his thing and he spends his whole life enjoying it. The president does his thing and goes through a grueling campaign to get to do what he does.

We all spend our time on *who* and *what* is most important to us.

We all spend our time on *who* and *what* we value most.

Yet at the moment we Americans find ourselves in a rather peculiar situation. Somehow, we find that time has been taken away from us. Time is no longer under our control. We find ourselves owned and controlled by our own way of life, a way of life that forces us to sacrifice our primary relationships to the mad velocity that controls the schedules of our daily lives.

Everyone's life has gone into overtime. Even school children don't have the time anymore to finish their homework. Children's homework, like our own work time, has gone into overload. Our overtime mode of working to support our deluxe way of living is depriving us of human time for human closeness.

A funny thing happened to us Americans on our way to success. In our sustained production of overabundant commodities, the less real—namely, material goods—has become more real, the really real—namely, ourselves and our loved ones—has become eliminated.

The passion that runs, rules, and ruins our lives is dispensing our time on disposable goods. We have lost our lives in a forest of products. To the sovereignty of consumer items we are forced to sacrifice our deepest relationships.

A mother works six days in the post office. On the seventh day she works as a waitress in a diner. Her husband works two jobs as well. They raise their children between work shifts. They say they have to do it to pay their bills.

Taking the Time to Love

Something is radically wrong if we have to put our family and children on hold in order to maintain our standard of living. Instead of drawing us closer together, the way we live is tearing us apart. The time has come to reassess what we Americans are doing with time, because what we are doing with time we are doing with our life.

Yet there is an alternative response to the exigencies of our existence if we keep in mind what Jesus did with time and how he used his time the way he did, giving persons the care that persons deserve, making possessions secondary to everything else in his life. Jesus initiated his followers into a way of life that was frugal and festive both. He showed them how it was possible to make do with less so they could enjoy themselves with one another an awful lot more.

We can only imagine what Jesus' evenings were like, drinking, dining, sharing jokes, telling stories, living a thrifty existence with friends, a life of the poor in spirit, and making our world know that the best things in life are free.

We learn from Jesus that riches are not needed for wealth. The little things that make us glad money can't buy. We can't buy a friend or a child. We can't pay for a great evening of laughing, dancing, and singing with the people we love. When it all comes down to what really matters, our deep connection to one another, our credit cards are useless.

The priceless gift of friends and family has no price. Money can't buy us love. The message of Jesus to America today is that we won't get love if we don't give love its time. We won't give love until we give love the time that all love takes. And to get back that kind of time we have to exit now off the commercial turnpike and do again what Jesus told us to do so long ago: *Put people first!*

Material goods be damned.

But [Jesus] answered, "It is written,
    'One does not live by bread alone,
        but by every word
        that comes from the mouth of God.'" . . .
    'Worship the Lord your God,
        and serve only him' " (Matthew 4:4, 10).

The Right Stuff

Moses said to the people, "Do not be afraid; for God has come only to test you and to put the fear of him upon you so that you do not sin" (Exodus 20:20).

THE DAY BEFORE Christmas there is a stampede of shoppers racing through our stores. The day after Christmas the stampede continues with the same intensity and force. No need to ask what our illness is! Our illness is our addiction to items of purchase, and the mad American imperative of having it all. The thrust of our whole existence is toward the raft of products we feel compelled to own in order to feel we are living the American way.

The point of existing according to our advertising world is driving around in an expensive car, wearing a Rolex watch, dressing in brand name clothes.

In this total advertising climate, showing off our personal belongings is an acceptable social practice. We present ourselves to others for their approval; we package ourselves in what's hot, what's cool, what's in, what's new. We all comply with this way of being American in our all-American world by flaunting our personal belongings. We depend on our possessions to earn the respect and admiration of others.

The right car
The right watch
The right sneakers
The right clothes
The right colors
The right match
The right mix
The right look
The right stuff!

Living as we are told to live, we are required to make ourselves look good. Men in the gym building muscle to look husky. Women in the beauty parlor making themselves up to look pretty. We are all dressing ourselves up; we are all making ourselves up; we are all building ourselves up. We are all looking to others to look at "us."

Nobody has told us the terrible truth that nobody is looking back. Nobody cares what clothes we wear as long as we wear something. If we wear nothing we will take away from what they are wearing.

The underlying, unacknowledged fact is that no one really gives a damn what kind of watch we wear, what kind of car we drive. Life in the fast lane means that no one has the time even to look sideways at anyone else. Everyone is so hassled and frazzled, so always in their own little dither, they cannot respond to anyone else's needs, still less attend to their own.

Looking to others to acknowledge who we are by what we own, the raw deal is that no one is looking back, because like ourselves they are up to their eyeballs in their own overwhelming world. We are all in this marathon together. For everyone around us the going way of doing life is doing life this way. There is no standpoint outside the madness to view how crazy, phony, and empty the whole thing is, except of course the Jesus take on doing life the Jesus way.

Jesus is so un-American and yet so contemporary in his message. Jesus makes more sense the more we see through the nonsense of our mad, commercial world. The gospel of Jesus does not sound foreign anymore once we acknowledge that our own way of life is foreign to what's real.

Fingering our way through the clothes rack in a big department store, looking for our size, we hear Jesus saying to us: *"Therefore I tell you, do not worry about your life, what you will eat or what you will drink, or about your body, what you will wear. Is not life more than food, and the body more than clothing?"* (Matthew 6:25) We say to ourselves, You know what? Jesus is right.

Health is on the way when we begin to get angry at our own stupidity and we ask ourselves out loud: Who are those few individuals from the garment industry who every season tell us, the masses, what to wear? And why do we just jump to the dress code they impose upon us and so submit to their control over us?

Why do we throw away all our good clothes to keep up with the tyranny of their ever-changing styles? Can we not dress as we like in our well-worn shoes and our well-loved clothes? Can we not share our hand-me-downs, give away to others the clothes we no longer need?

What is most frightening about our American standard of living is that we are sold on all options that are ours. We are told we are free to choose between forty brands of cereal, fifty kinds of sweaters, multiple kinds of automobiles loaded with all kinds of equipment. The only freedom we do not have is the greatest freedom of all. The freedom to say no; I don't want to live this life of consumption anymore.

All we have to do now is to make strides back to the school-house of Jesus and there become students again of his lifestyle of voluntary simplicity. *"Look at the birds of the air; they neither sow nor reap nor gather into barns, and yet your heavenly Father feeds them. Are you not of more value than they?"* (Matthew 6:26)

And so as asked by Jesus we leave the traffic to stop and give a look to such a simple sight as a bird building her simple nest. We watch her. She daubs the insides all around with mud, and she leaves a little pinhole in the bottom of her home to drain away the falling rain. Her homemaking, her housekeeping is done by the intuitive knack that makes her know how to make her world. If we watch her parenting her young we will catch her going out, and coming home with a worm or an insect in her mouth. At times she must be so hungry that she wants that worm for herself, but no, she is moved to forget herself and gives all of what she has to her little ones.

What can you call her giving if you do not call it love. The same love that makes the world make itself.

When we contrast the natural world of birds with our own human way of putting a roof over our heads, food in our bellies, clothes on our back, what strikes us as odd is that these doings of love, these things we do for one another, are tearing us apart.

The simple fidelity of being there to care for and feed one another that is the natural luxury of birds and animals is no longer an option for us Americans. So complex, so complicated, so convoluted is the commercial world we humans have created for ourselves.

We humans use our human brains differently than other animals. We call it creativity. We claim our creativity makes us special. We claim that creativity is the reason we are superior to all other species, and yet if we look at the world we human beings have created it is not about us humans at all. We humans are crazy out of control.

This is why Jesus asks us again to give a watch to the birds in their commercial-free world. And then turn back and take a look at ourselves to see *how the unreal has taken the place of the really real in our lives.*

From everyone to whom much has been given, much will be required; and from the one to whom much as been entrusted, even more will be demanded (Luke 12:48).

The Sum of Our Fears

Thus says the LORD:
Cursed are those who trust in mere mortals
    and make mere flesh their strength,
    whose hearts turn away from the LORD.
They shall be like a shrub in the desert,
    and shall not see when relief comes,
They shall live in the parched places of the wilderness,
    in an uninhabited salt land (Jeremiah 17:5–6).

DOWNSIZING THE SIGNIFICANCE of our material possessions and upscaling the significance of human persons, even when motivated by religious values, does not happen that easily. This is because as in the days of Jesus, it is our fears and not our religion that shapes and determines the way we meet our world. What, we ask, is it that we are so afraid of? The answer is that we are terrified of life.

Up from nothing, out of nowhere, here we are in this moment of time. Living a life that should never have happened in a universe that should never have been. If it were up to us we would not be at all. But here we are, nonetheless, in this strange passageway we are all traversing where the "I am" that we are goes on in "what is."

Life is blind. It comes to us from the blind side. We live in this blind spot. Life is a secret. We are that secret. No one knows what the secret is. We don't own life; life owns us. All we can do is surrender to this process of our coming up out of nothing and trust in tomorrow coming up out of nowhere while the "I am" that we are keeps going on in "what is."

Our fear of what we do not own and can't control is very human. We hold a very real dread over what it is that makes us be. We are clueless as to why we are here. It is not easy being human even if we are born that way. There is a hole of nothing-ness that opens up inside us that cannot be closed. We straddle a world supported by emptiness. We dangle above a great abyss. This is what scares the heck out of us.

There is no bedrock foundation upholding our existence. Life has no foothold. Our feet have no footing. There is no ground beneath this flow of day replacing day, coming from, passing by, going where, going, going, gone.

Nothing to hold, nothing to catch, nothing that lasts. In the undertow of life and time we lose our grip on what we cling to. Irreversible, inexplicable is the journey we are on; there is no escaping the burden of being alive. There is no way out of this odyssey we are on. A life that was always already on its way long before our time. We cannot run, duck, hide, deny, or avoid the debt we owe for being here.

Not to know life but to live it is our destiny; not to be sure of its outcome but to enter its mystery, this is our calling. There is no cure for our human condition. If life never spooks us, it is only because we don't want to know how spooky life is.

Life is frightening stuff. Fear is the emotion most natural to our human condition. Fear is the first feeling we feel when we are delivered from our mothers at birth. Fear is the last feeling we feel before death, knowing full well we will never come back.

Fear shadows us all the days of our life:

Fears of failure
Fears of not surviving
Fears of not being enough
Fears of our bosses
Fears of our teachers
Fears of losing our jobs
Fears of closeness
Fears of aloneness
Fears of not belonging
Fears of not belonging
Fears of not fitting in
Fears of how others will see us
Fears of what people will think of us
Fears of what people will say about us
Fears of those who are mad at us
Fears of what they will do to hurt us
Fears of failing in our most important relationships.

Behind our eyes, between our ears, down deep around the ribcage of our hearts, it is fear that makes or breaks our day.

We should never underestimate the psychological terror involved in being a human being. The overhead of us, the underneath of us, the beyond within us, the infinity between us, the yawning void that spontaneously creates, sustains, and carries us—it all scares the heck out of us.

The bottomless well of our human existence is not emotionally our most comfortable space for feeling at home. We don't go in for life. We bolt at the abyss that is our own within. So out we go looking to someone, or something other than us to give us security, safety, shelter, and life. We try hard to stay out of reality as it is by trying desperately to stay on top of things as they are.

We drown our primal feelings of holy terror in the ragtag busyness of everyday routines and rituals, chasing earthly dreams, running away from our earthly fears.

We organize life around our own gigs. Whatever we are up to, whatever we are into, whatever we are involved with, becomes such a big deal that all our emotions are wrapped around what we are doing.

Our Gee Whiz busyness lends substance to our otherwise groundless existence. We specialize in being special. We go for greatness in our field. We take control of our world by what we achieve. We use every gig to prove our worth. What we know, what we do, what we have, trumpets our own cosmic significance. The whole rigmarole of our everyday rat race helps us forget that we are candles in the wind, that we are building castles in the sand.

To avoid the terrible loneliness inside us that nothing takes away, we clutter our heads with the chatter of our audio-video world. To escape from the menace of our own inner emptiness we fill ourselves up by filling up our shopping bags.

We live in our heads away from our bodies. Our center is outside. We are plugged in to the world, tuned out on ourselves. Television, radios, cassette players are never shut off. We go all out for life's supply: movies, entertainment, sports, money, school, and work provide us with a sense of who we are. Telephone lines keep us tied to each other. Cellular phones ring forever.

It is the terror of real life that leads us human beings into reducing all reality into something as small as ourselves, something we can totally own and completely control. In other words, as I said previously, it is our fears that make us Americans reduce all living to money, school, shopping, and work, even to the point of neglecting everyone else, even to the point of neglecting to care for ourselves.

There are two sides to our human equation. There is our own side and then there is the God-side. We can, if we wish, live by fear and control out of our own side of life, or we can put our trust where trust belongs, in the God who brings us here.

Reaching into the depths of our own inner self we link our lives to God who began us, to God who carries us, to God who will forever hold us in God's forever love.

The guts of courage that come to human beings from their inner trust in God has always been greater in religious persons than their bowel-moving fears of life.

O LORD, my heart is not lifted up,
　　my eyes are not raised too high;
I do not occupy myself with things
　　too great and too marvelous for me.
But I have calmed and quieted my soul,
　　like a weaned child with its mother;
　　my soul is like the weaned child that is within me
(Psalm 131:1–2).

[Jesus] sent them out to proclaim the kingdom of God and to heal. He said to them, "Take nothing for your journey, no staff, nor bag, nor bread, nor money—not even an extra tunic. Whatever house you enter, stay there, and leave from there (Luke 9:2–4).

God or Apples?

Ho, everyone who thirsts,
come to the waters;
and you that have no money,
come, buy and eat!
Come, buy wine and milk
without money and without price.
Why do you spend your money for that which is not bread,
and your labor for that which does not satisfy?
Listen carefully to me, and eat what is good,
and delight yourselves in rich food.
Incline your ear, and come to me;
listen, so that you may live.
I will make with you an everlasting covenant (Isaiah 55:1–3).

IN THE GARDEN OF EDEN, Adam and Eve had to choose between God or apples. Afraid to live on God alone, they went for the apples. It has been for all of us God or apples ever since. Apples now being whatever addictions we need on the side, besides God, to handle our fears and anxieties of being alive.

Our tour of life through earth and time need not be exhausted by running from our fears. God in Jesus has revealed to us another way we can exist if we go into ourselves, not out to the world, for life.

God has given us all an inside place. It is the inner place that is our self. It is the one place that goes with us every place we go. It is our place of deepest feelings, where we feel feelings no one else feels. Day after day, year after year, for all of our lives, this is the place we never leave and, even when we sleep, it is where we dream. No one is us but us. We are our own stream of consciousness. Wherever we go, there we are. There is no hiding place from this hiding place, this inner space that is our very soul.

It is from out of this inner place that God in Jesus calls us now to live our lives. It was in there, in that desert soul of his own heart, that Jesus in prayer lived out his own life before the Father, in the Holy Spirit. Jesus calls us now to do the same.

There is something awfully lonely about this, our God calling, because it is the one thing each one of us must do for ourselves. As in all our other deep relationships, in our relationship with God there are degrees of closeness; there are degrees of distance.

Normally, we live our lives in and out of God, shifting from God awareness into total God forgetfulness. We pay God our *mini-visits*, a religious gesture now and then, but no surrender, no lasting change in the direction of our heart.

But then there comes a time for all of us when, from a half-life lived in God, we decide to give ourselves to God as Jesus showed us how! And when we do, God gives God to us, the more we give ourselves to God. We begin to feel within us God's presence, calling us always into deeper and deeper closeness.

Our awareness shifts from the outer world; we become more introspective. We find that life inside us is full of life if we give ourselves the time to live in there. The outer world begins to lose its hold on us. We no longer look to persons, places, or things to fill up our inner emptiness.

The world changes inside us humans, when we go inside, not

outside, for life. This sense of God's presence in us, we enter and leave, we feel and lose, but now we know—we find home within ourselves when we and God sit down to pray.

After a while, we want to be with God so much, we turn our lonely time into a time of prayer, we turn our aloneness into a chance to be with God. We go through life praying our way, each and every day. When our sense of self gets waffled by the outer world, when the world out there stirs up all our fears and sets off tiny terrors inside us, when we are all in a dither and bent out of shape, we know now from experience how praying always brings us back to our senses.

Inner togetherness always comes back to us whenever we and God sit down to talk things out.

If we are experiencing weakness, in prayer we soon experience strength.

If we are confused, in prayer we soon see the light.

If we are all torn up inside, in prayer we soon feel reconciled.

If we are discouraged, in prayer we soon take heart again.

In prayer we recover our center of gravity. In prayer we are made ready to take on the world again. We always emerge from our sessions with God with a renewed perspective on life. In prayer we remember what we humans forget. It is God, not ourselves, who brings us here.

Praying our way through life day by day by day, slowly but surely on many levels a foundational change takes place at the core of who we are. The "me" we were, is now a "we." We and God are now inseparable.

We live now, in a roomier world, where we ourselves are no longer the center of all that happens around us. We see care taking, not money making, now as our greatest human calling.

We live no longer in a world run by "me", but in a world loved by God. Our hearts have expanded, our horizons have widened. Our sensitivities have become more attuned to our own vulnerability and the divine beauty of all other human beings. We become:

Less righteous and more trusting
Less forceful and more nurturing
Less invasive and more respectful of other people's spaces
Less anxious and more peaceful
Less defensive and more open
Less separated and more connected,
Less consumers of products and more sharers of all that we have with others.

We learn for ourselves what every saint has ever told us, and what Jesus himself has shown us, that religion is simply our inner connection with God and our outer connection with one another.

What is God saying to us in sending us his only Son as one of our very own?

What is God in Jesus doing in our human world except calling us all to a monumental turning around of our lives, returning our human world back to a deep connection with him and close connection to others?

At that time Jesus said, "I thank you, Father, Lord of heaven and earth, because you have hidden these things from the wise and the intelligent and have revealed them to infants; ye, Father, for such was your gracious will. All things have been handed over to me by my Father; and no one knows the Son except the Father, and no one knows the Father except the son and anyone to whom the Son chooses to reveal him (Matthew 11:25–27).

The Sabbath As a Sharing Place

The LORD said to Moses: You yourself are to speak to the Israelites: "You shall keep my Sabbaths, for this is a sign between me and you throughout your generations, given in order that you may know that I, the LORD, sanctify you (Exodus 31:12–13).

TURNING OUR PLANET into a person-centered world is as much a religious endeavor today as it was in the days of Jesus. It puts one immediately into a countercultural posture.

The journey before us is terribly challenging and radically religious. Where do we find the space to get real about what is most real to us as religious persons except in the households of our own families.

In the Bible days of long ago, God asked the people then to declare for themselves a Sabbath. God wanted them to take a day for themselves, a day for one another, a day to tell the world to go away, a day to get away from it all.

Perhaps those people in those bygone times were losing touch with one another because, like ourselves, they too tended to lose themselves in the everyday busyness of taking a living from the world. Whatever God's reasons were for declaring a Sabbath, God's idea of a holy day for all human beings is a good idea for us Americans.

Setting right what has gone wrong for us means putting people first in our lives. And the place to begin this process is inside our own living quarters. What if, on some upcoming day, the whole family decided this is going to be our Sabbath?

We won't go to school
We won't go to work
We won't do anything all day
Today . . .

We'll take for ourselves a holiday of the heart so we can spend a crazy day together, finding out for ourselves, straight out from each other, how we feel about life inside us, how we feel about life between us.

Lounging around our homes in our bathrobes, dressed in ordinary duds, what if we vow to one another, starting here, starting now, that our home is no longer to be our flop house, where we all drop down dead tired at night in our beds, too exhausted to be bothered with anyone?

From here on in we decide that life within us and life between us comes first and foremost in the order of priorities. Education, work, income, and shopping will be necessary only in a secondary way to feed, clothe, and shelter ourselves.

Starting off our day of playing hooky from everything we are apt in the beginning to feel somewhat uneasy. What we run into is the stress of relaxing. Idleness does not come easy to us; we are not used to doing nothing together.

Breaking out of our routines to spend a day with one another we feel less safe, and a lot more unsure of ourselves. Without the usual background of television blaring, radio playing, and phone ringing, we suddenly feel uncomfortable as we struggle with closeness.

Doing nothing we feel like nothing, naked before each other. We are enveloped in an emptiness that is terribly threatening; we feel like bolting out the door. And yet, if we can stand the emptiness and hold the tension, the spontaneous will happen.

Feelings inside us, feelings between us, will surface. Feelings will speak now that feelings have a place to talk. Something new gets started in a setting that makes it normal and natural for us to interact with one another in a deep and open way.

Given the chance, given the time, given the place, we talk about ourselves, we talk about each other, we talk about our life together, before we know it we have a talkathon well underway. Our Sabbath has brought to the surface what's going on underneath. We deepen our relationships; we reach a new depth in our love for each other.

In the course of our Sabbath together we discover that not only do we need from time to time to take a holy day of the heart for ourselves, but we need as well to establish on a permanent basis a sharing place in our home.

We have all sorts of rooms in our homes—bedrooms, living rooms, dining rooms, laundry rooms, store rooms, bathrooms, television rooms—what we really need most of all is an encounter room.

A "can we talk" room, where each one feels free to speak straight up, straight out, and straight from the heart, the raw stuff going on within us and between us, without the fear of getting killed in the process. Every home needs such a pre-established place, permanently set aside for close encounters of the volatile kind, where the toxic elements in our relationships can be safely released.

Our human place of family love is a place of great intensity. Emotions shift and shift again, from situation to situation. In the push and pull of each other's influence, the needs and wants of others sometimes get frustrated. Unruly inner elements are frequently triggered. Love and hate rise not in turns but all at once and at the same time.

The strength of our relationships depends upon how we enter into and respond to each other's inner fields of changing emotions. This is why every home needs to set aside a special place where we can sit down together with love, not fear, and work out and work through the "roto rooter" stuff being passed back and forth between us.

What we need is nothing elaborate, just chairs facing each other, where we can sit across from one another and in the strength of our love allow ourselves to tell our life as it is, good and bad, in personal pronouns.

Something unlooked for always occurs when we turn our language loose and allow ourselves to speak freely. A big whopping love block stuck in somebody's throat is spontaneously aired, and a mutual attitude of humility, reverence, respect, is born again into our love affair.

Leaving the shallows to swim in the deep is the risk we take when we enter the field of another's feelings. There is nothing tidy or tied down about our life, when our love is lived at the level of speak out loud emotions. Yet when we are with one another, so totally vulnerable, so completely open, the dynamics are set in motion for growing in our love and deepening our intimacy.

Life gives us one another. We do our growing together. The inside story of our love story is told by ourselves as we move from day to day, to day. What we grow from, what we grow into, to a large extent depends so much upon how free we are with one another to say out loud what we deeply feel inside. What makes us religious persons, as Jesus has shown us, is how we are there for each other, how we are present to one another. This is what life is all about. Love is what we came here to do.

In our American system, the massive, pervasive, and persistent emphasis on education, occupation, and income skews life away from the importance of our relationships and puts love in our lives into total eclipse. It is precisely this misplaced emphasis that we have pumped into our way of life that is causing us to lose touch emotionally with ourselves, and lose out on each other.

From here to eternity, or at least for a very long time, putting what matters back into proper perspective will be our ongoing constant uphill struggle. This is why every family must create its own holy day, and every household establish within its walls a meeting place where relationships are again and again restored to their rightful place as the center of our whole existence.

Beloved, since God loved us so much, we also ought to love one another. No one has ever seen God; if we love one another, God lives in us, and his love is perfected in us (1 John 4:11–12).

Love is patient; love is kind; love is not envious or boastful or arrogant or rude. It does not insist on its own way; it is not irritable or resentful; it does not rejoice in wrongdoing, but rejoices in the truth. It bears all things, believes all things, hopes all things, endures all things (1 Corinthians 13:4–7).

Honest-to-God Conversation

As God's chosen ones, holy and beloved, clothe yourselves
with compassion, kindness, humility, meekness, and patience.
Bear with one another and, if anyone has a complaint
against another, forgive each other; just as the Lord has
forgiven you, so you also must forgive (Colossians 3:12–13).

PSYCHOTHERAPY IS CALLED the talking cure. Some
critics call it expensive conversation. Its art is very simple:
someone listens attentively to someone else speaking honestly.
Must Jesus come back again to remind us that, of all the gifts we
have to give, nothing could be greater than offering ourselves to
be there for one another?

In that most human of encounters, one person listening to
another person speaking, the emotional knots in which the
speaker is hopelessly entangled become unraveled and he or she
is freed up inside to live a fuller life.

All our contemporary counseling therapies confirm the fact
that there is healing and health, wellness and wholeness, when
we take the time for talking to each other honestly and listening
to each other attentively.

The crime against our own humanity that we Americans are
now committing is this: the time we spend in making a living

deprives us of the time for this most human luxury of all, the time for honest-to-God human conversation.

In the real world of real people, every moment, real feelings are felt. We have a great need to share these feelings with the ones who figure deeply in our lives. This is what intimacy is all about; this is what relationships are for—everything else we do for ourselves.

What we are missing out on, in our fast-track existence, is the timeless chance we have in the here and now to get inside each other's head, to move inside each other's heart, to live inside each other's life, by taking the time to get to know the inner stuff going on inside us all the time. And this is the only place where real life is taking place all the time.

No matter how old we are, no matter how young we are, we all need to hear from another human being:

I hear you!
I see you!
I am with you!

We all need someone to say "wow" to our existence. As human beings we have this fundamental need to let another human being into what's going on inside us all the time. We cannot see ourselves. We need others to mirror for us who we are. Hearing ourselves heard, seeing ourselves seen, knowing that we are known, we are no longer alone in our own little world. Our separateness is overcome, our uniqueness confirmed, in our bodily-felt feeling of oneness with others.

When we understand each other well, when we are on each other's side, then is when we feel connected, related, and at home. The depth of our humanity we come to experience only as insiders inside each other's inner journey.

In our being together with one another there is the constant coming to know ourselves.

Leaving our own world to enter the world of another, a new world of love is always coming into being.

In the soul-making moments of our soul-making contacts, something new is happening every moment.

We leave where we were. We enter where they are. We come away always totally different. The greatest of all human events occurs where we meet deeply with one another, and where we are met in depth.

Being there, to the "there" of another. There is where we experience how much more there is to life. In other words, there we experience God. Buried deep in the essentials of our humanity is this awful yearning, this infinite longing, for deep, reliable, ongoing, life-long, time-consuming intimacy with others.

Once we acknowledge that human life is human closeness with our loved ones, then new issues are raised about our own way of life as a consumer society. Our endless itchy frenzy buying and disposing of commodities begins to feel loathsome, especially when we recognize that it is precisely this garbage in and garbage out process that has come between ourselves and the ones who mean the world to us.

But Jesus called them to him and said, "You know that the rulers of the Gentiles lord it over them, and their great ones are tyrants over them. It will not be so among you; but whoever wishes to be great among you must be your servant, and whoever wishes to be first among you must be your slave" (Matthew 20:25–27).

Life by a Different Rule

For thus said the Lord GOD, the Holy One of Israel:
In returning and rest you shall be saved;
  in quietness and in trust shall be your strength
(Isaiah 30:15).

LIFE WOULD BE a different game, played by different rules if we followed the festive, frugal way of Jesus that makes persons, not products, the centerpiece of our whole existence. Seeing our world through the eyes of Jesus we see the need to take back what we are giving away to keep up with our way of life. What we need to reclaim is nothing extraordinary, but something as normal and as natural as our family meals.

Fast foods, fast pace, fast life in the fast lane have done away with those moments around the family table so pivotal to our human closeness. Human beings forever before us sat down together to eat. They laughed, talked, shouted, argued with one another while sharing their food. They bonded and connected through the volatile, visceral interaction of their family meal.

It is not the frozen dinner heated up in a microwave oven that warms the cockles of the human heart and gives a feeling of closeness to another. No, it is the sit-down long-drawn-out family dinners where everyone has a chance to spit out to one another where they are coming from inside.

More than with food, we feed one another with our presence. Family table talk is like splitting the atom; everyone releases energy and vitality. When we celebrate our common life around the family table we make our household into a lived-in place; each one of us brings exciting and different specialties to our home life if we make the time to be at home.

Making important what is important requires shifting the focus of family life back to our family spaces where we make the time, and take the time, to find out for ourselves how it feels to be that somebody else who shares with us our living quarters. Returning our earth to a person-centered planet after the model of Jesus is not a cosmic, messianic endeavor. It is a project as local as our living room, or our dining room.

We all live within the superdome of a great big television bubble. Its flickering blue lights are everywhere. Its numbing, dumbing, drumming sounds render us brain-dead to real life. It is amazing how much our family life has been taken away from us by this big-mouth, mindless chatterbox that has taken over all our conversations and reduced our families to muted silence.

How passive we active Americans have become when we are reduced to couch potatoes, voyeurs who peep at the peep shows of others living life. There on the small screen we watch other humans relating to one another, minds shut to the living, breathing, feeling humans sitting on the couch right next to us.

We are spoken for. We do not speak. We withdraw our interest in each other while we invest time and attention on audio sounds and video images of a prerecorded existence. It is like going out to dinner and never talking to one another, just listening to the conversation of the people at the table right next to us.

Making important what is important will bring our world back to the real world of our life together to one another. Great indeed will be the vitality in our living quarters when we make our homes an open house, a truth-telling space where life is emotional and living is relational. Turning away from the canned life of prerecorded entertainment to life inside us and life between us will make such a difference in the quality of our existence with one another.

Who needs talk shows when we begin talking to one another again?

Who needs sitcoms when we make our own homes houses of our own fun?

Who needs soap operas when our own lives are more conflicted and complicated, also more interesting, than any other life ever was or ever could be?

Who needs chat rooms if we can talk and listen again to our own loved ones?

Once we begin first-hand living, then we can give up our second-hand lifestyle. Homemade songs, homemade meals, homemade fun, homemade games, homemade clothes will free us from our dependence upon the mass media telling us how we should live and what we must buy to keep up with an alienating lifestyle.

Once upon a time, once upon our world, there was a man named Saint Francis. He lived in Assisi, Italy. His problems were the same as our problems now. In his life, like it is in our life, the secondary aspects of his existence had become his primary concerns. Those things which should have come first had fallen back into second place. Saint Francis said phooey to the system.

"Phooey" is the "bad word" saints always use when saints get fed up with our worldly systems. Francis the womanizer, Francis the rowdy soldier, Francis the trendy clothes lover, turned it all around to become like Jesus, a hugger of lepers and a server of humans. Our calling, like his calling, is calling us all to convert to a modest sufficiency in lifestyle so that we can enjoy again the closeness to others we so desperately long for.

And what do we need to reclaim but

Family time,
> *Meal time,*
>> *Prayer time,*
>>> *Together time,*
>>> *Love time,*
>>>> *Time to make love to our spouses,*
>>>>> *Time to grow up with our kids?*

But we have this treasure in clay jars, so that it may be made clear that this extraordinary power belongs to God and does not come from us. We are afflicted in every way, but not crushed; perplexed, but not driven to despair; persecuted, but not forsaken; struck down, but not destroyed; always carrying in the body the death of Jesus, so that the life of Jesus may also be made visible in our bodies (2 Corinthians 4:7–10).

What's a Parent to Do?

. . . for love is strong as death,
passion fierce as the grave.
Its flashes are flashes of fire,
a raging flame.
Many waters cannot quench love,
neither can floods drown it (Song of Solomon 8:6–7).

NO ONE DOES parenting better than parents. Without being told, every child already knows how much they're worth by how much time their parents spend with them. The amount of time their parents give them tells them clearly that they matter to them more than anything else is their parents' world.

In that human moment of a parent meeting a child getting off the school bus, you have the greatest demonstration of what parental love on earth is all about.

Parenting is leaving our own world to enter the world of our child so that we can be with them in their world. The interior life of a child is accessible to us only when we take the time to allow them to speak as we give them a listen. It is a shock to discover how simple and human is this gift of love parents give their children.

Parenting is paying the full respect of our total attention to our children, listening to them in such a way that we feel their whole experience.

Parenting is being with a child who is trying to tell us who he is, who she is.

Parenting is reaching out to what's going on in their lives. It is the submission of ourselves to the suchness of their world.

Parenting is an attitude of openness and acceptance to the way children come to us from wherever they are coming, allowing all that's inside them to come out in the open.

Parenting is a total devotion to the uniqueness that each child is.

Parenting is knowing every human brain has a mind of its own and every human child has something special to say if someone special is there to listen.

Parenting is wanting to know who is the one inside those eyes, who is the one behind those smiles, who is the mysterious mischievous person present to us here and now, sometimes happy, sometimes sad, sometimes laughing, sometimes crying.

Parenting is taking our children into our hearts by giving them ourselves, offering them the chance to be completely themselves.

Parenting is a sacred space of total trust and naked honesty where parents give their child the most precious gift of all, the gift of their own sense of self.

Parenting is the role parents play for God in the self-becoming of another human being.

Parents not only give their children their bodies. Parents also give their children their souls, for through and only through their parents' parenting them do children ever get to know themselves. No other way is there for children to reach their innermost, own-most, God-most selves except through their parents' parenting them.

In heaven it is the Holy Trinity of the Father, Son, and Holy Spirit; on earth for every child the holy trinity is Daddy, Mommy and me.

What do children want?
    Parents!

What do parents want?
    Children!

What do they both want?
    Time to spend together,
        for deep connection
        with one another.

This is the kind of time our way of life will never give them.
    So they take the time,
        and make the time,
        no matter the consequences.

People were bringing even infants to him that he might touch them; and when the disciples saw it, they sternly ordered them not to do it. But Jesus called for them and said, "Let the little children come to me, and do not stop them; for it is to such as these that the kingdom of God belongs. Truly I tell you, whoever does not receive the kingdom of God as a little child will never enter it (Luke 18:15–17).

Getting a Head Start
for Our Children

And as for me, this is my covenant with them, says the
LORD: my spirit that is upon you, and my words that I have
put in your mouth, shall not depart out of your mouth, or
out of the mouths of your children, or out of the mouths of
your children's children, says the LORD, from now on and
forever (Isaiah 59:21).

WE ARE A DRIVEN people. We drive ourselves. We drive one
another. In every aspect of our lives as Americans we tend to be
coercive. Raising cattle, growing plants, we pour chemicals into
our products to force growing and speed up ripening. But in our
hurry we poison everything.

We haven't done much better by our kids in the way we
educate them.

Rushed ourselves, we pressure them. We force their growth;
we hurry their childhood. As soon as they can see, we teach them
to read. As soon as they can walk, we crowd them with educa-
tional toys. Before they know what's happening they are
calculating with calculators, computing with computers. The
message is subtle. No one says it; the heat is on. We exert

pressure to "head start" them and get them going down the learning road.

Being of good intent, of course, we only want to give our kids a jump on life. All our intensity is poured into education. The folk wisdom of our folk ways goes unquestioned, goes like so—kids who do well in school do well in life.

What goes unsaid, but is clearly understood, is that childhood is not the real world. The real world is up ahead. Away out there somewhere where adults know what life is all about.

Life is never where our children are. So early on they learn that the present is useless and must always be sacrificed to someone else's idea of their future. So school is the place where children are taught to believe above all in our system, and in doing so they no longer believe in themselves.

In school they learn to sacrifice their real self in order to get by in the real world.

Why can't the school day begin where the children are?

Why can't school center on persons instead of brains?

Why can't school be the "wow" of discovery rather than the yawn that it is?

Why can't school be an easy, friendly place instead of a pressure cooker where children chew on their fingers and bite their nails? Why?

Because it is not the way of our American mindset to wait upon a child, leaving open the outcome of his or her growing, trusting that there is a way in each child that finds its own way if we get out of their way. Trusting in the original blessing that they are, believing in the suchness of all that is in them, allowing the seed of their own personality to come to its own full size in its own peculiar way in its own good time. Each child would grow so naturally to be themselves if we did not insist so much on how they ought to grow.

We steamroll over their existing now. We extinguish who they are and replace their present person with the promise of some future someone we hope they will become through education. We force them into skipping childhood. Forever they will suffer for that missing element in their development.

May the ways we educate give way to another way of educating, the way of connecting with each child.

Schools designed to make room and time for every little child to beget their little self, leaving no one and nothing out.

Schools that believe in children and the almighty resources that come with them each day to school.

Schools convinced there is a little self in there hiding in every child. The little face doesn't say it all.

Every child is a many-sided individual. It depends which side you are looking for. Given the right environment, accepted fully, the mystery persons there will step out on the floor someday, knowing that everyone can be trusted with something as precious as the total showing of one's total self. Schools where children are made to feel that they as persons are the primary element in education will grow up to be adults who make human beings more important in their lives than anything else.

Our schools must change if we want our children to learn young and early that they as persons are what life is all about.

Lucky the children and happy their childhood who have parents who believe making a living is much less important than making a life. Led by their hearts not by their fears such parents feel no need to lay some plans of future success on their children's present time. They honor their children's experience by taking part in how their children discover the world; they are parents who kid around, sit around while their children grow, allowing them to dilly dally on their way, with minimum interference.

These parents enable their becoming to follow its natural course and take its own sweet time; they wait out their children's searchings and their findings until they find out who they are themselves and what they want from life.

Over the years, life becomes fun between parent and child. Fears are replaced with mutual trust. The need to control yields to mutual respect. Life is easy where love is free and no one lays on another their ideas of what the other should be. Everyone grows where parents and children grow together. Insiders inside each other's journey with no agenda except their presence to each other's presence.

If we wish to return our planet to a person-centered world then we will give our children back their childhood. As we live our lives respecting them as persons they will live their lives respecting others.

As we enjoy their childhood they will enjoy the childhood of their children. The world changes only when we ourselves change the way we live in our own families.

> *Jesus answered him, "Very truly, I tell you, no one can enter the kingdom of God without being born of water and Spirit. What is born of the flesh is flesh, and what is born of the Spirit is spirit. Do not be astonished that I said to you, 'You must be born from above.' The wind blows where it chooses, and you hear the sound of it, but you do not know where it comes from or where it goes. So it is with everyone who is born of the Spirit"* (John 3:5–8).

At that time the disciples came to Jesus and asked, "Who is the greatest in the kingdom of heaven?" He called a child, whom he put among them, and said, "Truly I tell you, unless you change and become like children, you will never enter the kingdom of heaven. Whoever becomes humble like this child is the greatest in the kingdom of heaven (Matthew 18:1–4).

Courage is Fear Overcome by Faith

For I, the LORD your God,
    hold your right hand;
it is I who say to you, "Do not fear,
    I will help you" (Isaiah 41:13).

. . . I have set before you life and death, blessings and curses.
Choose life so that you and your descendants may live,
loving the LORD your God, obeying him, and holding fast to
him (Deuteronomy 30:19–20).

OUR WAY OF LIFE would have us give each other things, when all we really want from one another is the giving of ourselves. The strength of any organization, business, or institution depends upon its credibility when our American system becomes questionable. Then all the energy invested in it slowly leaks away.

It is in our guts where we first get the feeling that something is horribly wrong with our American living arrangements. As our growing self-knowing keeps on growing, we move through four gradual states of alienation as we fall out of love with our way of life.

- *Stage 1*

  We live each day overwhelmed in nervous exhaustion, anxiety, and tension. In our everyday existence we feel swamped by the impossible demands constantly coming at us from everywhere all around us. We feel like a boiler about to explode. Everyone else seems to be able to cope with the stress. We begin to get down on ourselves, asking What's wrong with me? In this stage of emotional turmoil we are still blaming ourselves for not being able to fit into our outfit. We feel the fault lies in us, not in the system. We are the ones who are inadequate. We are the ones who have lost our edge. We are the ones who can no longer go the distance or keep up with the pace.

- *Stage 2*

  This is the stage of self-righteous rage. This is the stage in which we discover that it is not us that is inadequate—it is the whole damn system that is dysfunctioning. It is the system that has pushed us into this corner of impossible demands. We know now why we are taking a beating. It is our whole way of life that is crazy, not us.

- *Stage 3*

  It is a more humble space to be in. In our honest-to-God moments we admit to ourselves that we are the ones who participate in, contribute to, and benefit from the system, even though we now realize that, in living out a way of life so organized by others for us, we wind up living a way of life that is working against us.

  In other words we are the ones using the system so we cannot blame the system if the system is also using us. In pure desperation we wind up in a do-or-die struggle trying to control a marketing setup that's out to control us. When we feel used up, overworked, overwhelmed, burned out, shut down, withdrawn, we must acknowledge that no one is doing this to us—we are doing this to ourselves.

There is nothing mysterious at all about the free-floating rage we sense all around us—air rage, work rage, road rage, home rage, desk rage. It is telling us something about the way we have organized our lives. And it is as simple as this: We humans get angry when someone else does a number on us. What we seem to forget is that we also get angry whenever we are doing a number on ourselves.

If we are mad at the world these days, it is only because we are really ticked off with ourselves. As we scream and moan about our situation, as we cast about looking for a scapegoat to blame for where we are, let us keep the accusing finger pointing straight at nothing else except at that old devil inside us that makes us shop until we drop. It is not the system that is beating us up. It is the side effects of buying, buying, buying that keep hurting us so bad. Simply put, we are overspending and so we are forever physically, emotionally, financially always overspent. Nothing will ever change that until we undergo a life changing change in ourselves.

- ### *Stage 4*

From bitching about the system, like Moses, we switch. We are willing to live out of the God-side of this side of life.

When God in Jesus announced his mission to our planet, he said he had come to "proclaim release to the captives" and "to let the oppressed go free" (Luke 4:18). We Americans are reluctant to admit that we are prisoners to our zany mania for buying, obtaining, owning, and having everything that imprisons us in the prison house of helpless, hopeless, powerless economic captives.

God's plaintive plea to us in Jesus is his begging us to realize that there is a lot more to life than just commercial products. The teachings of Jesus look easy on paper, but in practice they are as radical now as they were way back then. The full measure of Jesus' plan for our human happiness is a changing of our sense of what matters.

When for religious reasons we make our ministry to one another our primary commitment, then one cup, one plate, one spoon, one fork, one knife, one chair will do for each one of us. If this is what it takes to take back our lives for love's sake, then this is what it takes.

We cannot ask that our world be about persons unless we ourselves move to make persons the center of our own world. This is the last and greatest freedom left to us as Americans, the freedom to create a person-friendly world, friendly to persons in our own person-friendly households.

For families willing to commit themselves to such a radical restructuring of their existence this book is written, to start the conversation of how our human living can be done, otherwise than the way we do our living now. It is a mission akin to David up against Goliath, but then again our strength is in our god. courage is our fears overcome by our faith.

For surely I know the plans I have for you, says the LORD, plans for your welfare and not for harm, to give you a future with hope. Then when you call upon me and come and pray to me, I will hear you (Jeremiah 29:11–12).

And [Jesus] replied, "Who are my mother and my brothers?" And looking at those who sat around him, he said, "Here are my mother and my brothers! Whoever does the will of God is my brother and sister and mother" (Mark 3:33–35).

Scripture Index